young people of south asia

R

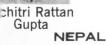

chitri Rattan
Gupta

NEPAL

ndira Devi
Chalise

Man Bahadur
Lama

BURMA

Khin Maung
Win

May May
Kyaing

PAKISTAN

THAILAND

Najma Yusuf

Tipawan
Thamthiangsat

Phiboon
Saskuan

CEYLON

MALAYA

Ramani
Witanachchi

Nihal
Dissanayake

Mariati bt. Aziz

Tan Poay Lim

Young People
of
South Asia

BOOKS BY CHARLES R. JOY

Young People of Western Europe
Young People of Central Europe
Young People of the British Isles
Young People of the Eastern Mediterranean
Young People of the Western Mediterranean
Young People of West Africa
Young People of East and South Africa
Young People of the Pacific Islands
Young People of East Asia and Australia
Young People of South Asia
Young People of Mexico and Central America
Young People of South America
Young People of the West Indies
Africa: A Handbook for Travelers
Emerging Africa: A Scholastic World Affairs Multi-Text
Light in the Dark Continent: People of the African Equator
Island in the Desert: Challenge of the Nile Valley
Desert Caravans: Challenge of the Changing Sahara
Taming Asia's Indus River: Challenge of Dust, Drought, and Flood
The Race Between Food and People: Challenge of a Hungry World
Getting to Know Israel
Getting to Know the Two Chinas
Getting to Know the South Pacific
Getting to Know Hong Kong
Getting to Know the Sahara
Getting to Know Tanzania
Getting to Know the Amazon
Getting to Know the Tigris and Euphrates
Getting to Know El Salvador, Nicaragua, and Costa Rica
Getting to Know England, Scotland, Ireland, and Wales
The Africa of Albert Schweitzer (co-author)
The Animal World of Albert Schweitzer
Music in the Life of Albert Schweitzer
Wit and Wisdom of Albert Schweitzer

Young People
of
South Asia

THEIR STORIES IN THEIR OWN WORDS

by
CHARLES R. JOY

MEREDITH PRESS
New York

First Edition

YOUNG PEOPLE OF SOUTH ASIA was originally published in 1964 over the imprint of Duell, Sloan and Pearce, an affiliate of Meredith Press.

Grateful acknowledgment is made to **Junior Scholastic**, the magazine in which some of these stories have been published in a different and briefer form. Other stories appear here for the first time.

Library of Congress Catalogue Card Number: 64-12451

Manufactured in the United States of America for Meredith Press

CONTENTS

Note: The countries of Viet Nam, Cambodia, Singapore, and Indonesia are included in *Young People of East Asia and Australia.* Jordan, Lebanon, Israel, and Turkey are included in *Young People of the Eastern Mediterranean.*

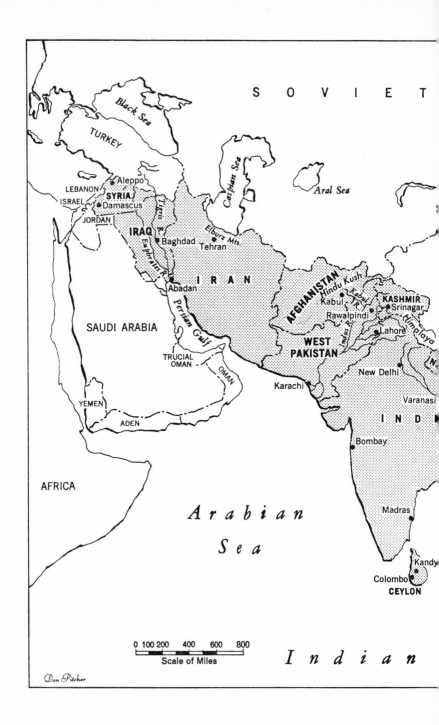

FOREWORD

There was a time when the western world did not know even the direction in which the fabled lands of Asia lay. Columbus sailed westward across the Atlantic with a letter to deliver to the Grand Khan of China. He reached Central America. Henry Hudson sailed north on the river that was named for him. He was not trying to reach Albany, where his little ship went aground. His objective was Canton in China. Magellan sailed south on his extraordinary voyage round the world, hoping to find a strait in the South Atlantic through which he could pass on his way to the gold and spices of the Orient. Vasco da Gama rounded the Cape of Good Hope and sailed eastward, finally reaching India, the land of which the great Portuguese navigators had dreamed.

Today no one has to sail into the perilous unknown any more to find the Far East. We can draw accurate maps of it.

We used to travel to Asia on lovely clipper ships like the *Flying Cloud*, the big, white sails on their tall, graceful spars bulging in the wind. Then the steamer came. To the natives in far lands they were demons belching black smoke. Then came the clipper planes that took off and landed on the water, so big that they had sitting rooms, dining rooms, kitchens, and a long compartment in the tail fitted with pullman bunks. With the development of large fuel tanks, other heavier-than-air planes like the Constellation began to fly the oceans, making long jumps from land to land. And now we have the speedy jets that lengthen the daylight hours to set us down in the Far East in an amazingly short space of time.

The world is shrinking in size.

Yet, to us westerners, Asia is still a very strange, complex, confusing continent. It is all the more so because it is changing so rapidly. It was Tennyson who wrote: "The old order changeth, yielding place to new." Nowhere is this more true than in the world of southern Asia, which we shall visit in this book. The day of foreign domination has almost completely disappeared. A new free world is being born.

If you want to know what this new world will be like in the future you cannot do better than listen to these young people who will help to shape it. You will begin to understand their nations better as you see them through their eyes.

What an interesting and varied group they are: a Thai classical dancer, a novice in a Buddhist monastery, the daughter of a Hindu priest, the son of an Arab sheikh, a Moslem girl from the vale of Kashmir, twins from the capital of Afghanistan!

This is the ninth book in our young people's series. Our world family grows steadily bigger. It's a united family too, striving together to bring friendship and peace through understanding.

Young People
of
South Asia

1. SOUTH ASIA

DARING ADVENTURES

One-third of the earth and two-thirds of the people of the earth are in Asia. Those who know that part of the globe say, "It's a whale of a continent!" Yet for long centuries Asia was very remote from the civilizations of the Mediterranean. It took very daring and hardy adventurers to visit this region, and there were few of them.

The most famous of all was Marco Polo, the Venetian traveler, who was struck with wonder by the splendor he found at the court of the Khan of China. He visited Southeast Asia, India, and other places in this great area. He lived in the latter part of the thirteenth and the beginning of the fourteenth centuries.

Another extraordinary traveler was a Moslem from Tangier. His name was Ibn Batuta, and for thirty years he wandered over the world. He never met Marco Polo, for his travels probably began a year or two after Polo's death; but his journeys were more extensive than Polo's or any other traveler's in the Middle Ages. He not only visited China and India but also Ceylon, Indonesia, Asia Minor, Syria, Arabia, Mesopotamia, and Persia. He is not so well known as Marco Polo because his writings were only discovered when the French occupied Algeria.

MOUNTAIN AND DESERT BARRIERS

Asia is six thousand miles wide, stretching from the Mediterranean to the Pacific. Between the Mediterranean countries and the countries of South Asia there were (and, of course, still are) big, waterless deserts and high ice-tipped mountains. You could reach India in those days only through the passes of the Hindu Kush. The name of these mountains means the Hindu-Killer, for the Hindus who tried to climb them often perished.

The best known of the passes through which the early traders and invaders of India toiled is the Khyber Pass up on the northwest frontier. This pass is forty miles long and lies 6,825 feet above the sea. The inviting plains of India were open to those who could fight their way through this gap in the Hindu Kush.

Far in the north, mountain ranges like the Pamirs and the Himalayas protect South Asia from attack. To the east, of course, was the formidable barrier of the greatest ocean in the world. It isn't strange that South Asia in particular was so hard to reach.

THE EUROPEANS COME

Toward the end of the fifteenth century the Europeans first came to Asia. They arrived by sea, and they were seeking what they believed to be the wealth of the Orient. This wealth at the beginning consisted mostly of spices. There was no refrigeration in Europe in those days, so the spices were very useful for covering the bad taste of spoiling meats and other foods. After this first voyage the European ships came in greater and greater numbers.

THE PENINSULAS OF SOUTH ASIA

The land mass that extends from the Atlantic to the Pacific is called Eurasia. Asia is the greater part of it, and Europe is simply a big peninsula extending from the central mass out to the west. India is another great peninsula, almost as large as Europe. To the east of India are two more peninsulas. The peninsula of Indo-China is occupied by the countries of Viet Nam, Cambodia, Laos, Thailand, and Burma. South of this peninsula the long, narrow Malay Peninsula stretches for about a thousand miles like a snake with the egg of Singapore in its mouth. Over to the west in South Asia is the Arabian Peninsula, so arid in the interior that not a single stream flows there the year round.

A GEOGRAPHICAL EXPRESSION

Some of the countries in the southeast have been included in the book of this series called *Young People of East Asia and Australia*. Others in the west fall naturally within the limits of *Young People of the Eastern Mediterranean*. In between are a dozen countries where the young people of the present book live.

We shall have much to say about these countries as one by one we reach them in our travels. But not so much can be said of South Asia as a whole. South Asia is simply a geographical term and nothing else. The words have no other meaning.

This big and fascinating part of our globe's surface has no unity of any kind save that of geography.

THE ROOF OF THE WORLD

Geographically, however, there are many interesting things to be said about it. Take the mountains, for instance. Those in the north of Nepal, India, Pakistan, and Afghanistan are the highest, the most rugged, and yet the youngest mountains on the globe. They are so lofty that we call them the "Roof of the World." The highest mountain in the world, Mount Everest, is here, 29,028 feet in altitude.

Yet these soaring citadels of the sky rise from what was once long ago a great sea, longer and wider than the Mediterranean. This was the Tethys. It was formed during the paleozoic and the mesozoic eras. The words mean ancient life and middle life and they refer to the third and fourth periods in geologic time. Gradually this sea filled with sediment, and then there came some great upheaval of the earth with tremendous pressure from the north which forced these mighty mountains up into the heavens. It was at this time that the Himalayas, the Karakoram, the Pamirs, the Hindu Kush, and other ranges were born.

STORIED RIVERS

Then from the snows and glaciers that formed up there in the cold air miles above, the sea streams began to flow, seeking their way southward to the plains. They gouged out canyons in the midst of the mountains, gorges sometimes two miles deep. The streams ran together to form great rivers—some of them among the mighty ones of the earth. The Indus and its great branches carved their way to the Arabian Sea through Tibet, India, Pakistan, and Afghanistan. The holy river of the

Hindus, the Ganga (or Ganges), ran down through the plains of India, past the sacred city of Benares, which the people call Varanasi, and then flowed through the many branches of its swampy East Pakistan delta to empty into the Bay of Bengal. The Tigris and the Euphrates, cradled in the mountains of Turkey, journeyed on to irrigate the thirsty lands of Syria and Iraq until they poured their mingled waters into the Persian Gulf.

ANCIENT CIVILIZATIONS

On the banks of these fertile rivers, which were the life blood of the earth, people settled in little communities, and civilizations were born. Some of the oldest culture centers in the world sprang up in these river valleys. Babylonia flourished in the lower valley formed by the Tigris and Euphrates from the third millennium to the middle of the first millennium B.C.

Up in the north of present-day Iraq on the Tigris River another mighty, ancient civilization took shape at just about the same time. This was Assyria. Its capital was at first Ashur and later Nineveh. Great kings ruled this empire, some of whom we read about in the Bible: Sargon, Sennacherib, Esar-Haddon, Assurbanipal.

Another extraordinary ancient civilization appeared in the valley of the Indus. It was somewhat younger than Assyria and Babylon, but it rose quite independently, producing its own written language and its own high culture.

MANY DIFFERENT STOCKS

From these old civilizations, from the invaders who conquered the lands and intermarried with the people they found there, from the Europeans who came as traders, rulers, teachers, and missionaries and settled among the natives, many different stocks have taken shape, each with its own language, its own customs, its own traditions. As we travel from country to country we find many differences, and even within a single land a surprising number of variations. There are, for instance, hundreds of languages in India alone.

WORLD RELIGIONS

Many of the great religions of the world were born in South Asia. Christianity appeared there; its holy shrines stand today in Nazareth, Bethlehem, and Jerusalem. Judaism was born there, for Abraham came from Ur in Iraq and Moses from the southern deserts. The prophets, the law-givers, the kings, the poets of Israel lived, labored, and died near the valley of the Jordan. Islam came to life there, and Mecca and Medina in Arabia, Jerusalem in Jordan, and Damascus in Syria cherish the four great Moslem mosques. Buddhism arose there, for Buddha was born in Nepal, and first taught his doctrine in India. Hinduism was born there and became the religion of the great majority of the Indian people. It has many gods and goddesses, many cults and different practices. Hinduism is not only a religion; it is also a philosophy, a complete way of life. Zoroastrianism grew there, first taught by a religious sage called Zoroaster. Its followers are still found in Iran and India. There were other sects too, like the Jains, and the Sikhs. No great religion has ever made its first appearance outside of Asia, and most of them were born in South Asia.

LOVELY TEMPLES

The great temples of religion are everywhere. At Varanasi on the holy river there are thousands of Hindu temples. A few miles away at Sarnath is the place where Buddha preached his first sermon to a few of his former disciples. This is the birthplace of Buddhism. Bangkok, the capital of Thailand, is full of wonderful places of worship: the Temple of the Emerald Buddha within the palace grounds, the Temple of Dawn rising majestically on the banks of the Menam River; the Temple of the Reclining Buddha, and the Marble Temple. One-fifth of the area of the whole big city is covered by temples and temple grounds.

So it is with all these countries. Malaya has the Million Buddhas Precious Pagoda in Penang. Burma has the Shwe Dagon, the loftiest Buddhist temple in the world. Ceylon has its Temple of the Tooth, where one of Buddha's teeth is venerated. West Pakistan has at Lahore the largest Moslem mosque in the world. A few miles away across the Indian border is the Golden Temple of the Sikhs at Amritsar. Syria has the Mosque of Omayyad, where the head of John the Baptist is said to be cherished. Jordan has the Dome of the Rock in Jerusalem, a place sacred to Christians, Jews, and Moslems alike. Saudi Arabia has Mecca and Medina, cities that Mohammed made holy. Israel has Nazareth, where Jesus grew to manhood, and the Sea of Galilee, by the shores of which Jesus gathered his disciples.

But the most wonderful of all these religious shrines is the Taj Mahal at Agra, India, built by the great Mogul emperor, Shah Jehan, as a tomb for his beloved wife, who was the "jewel of the palace."

FARMERS

The people who worship at these many temples and live near the life-giving rivers are mostly farmers. The main crop in the south of this region is rice, in the north wheat; but many other crops are also harvested. The farmers depend on the rains and the streams for water. Up to four thousand miles east of the Atlantic, most of the rain comes from that ocean. Farther east most of it comes from the Indian Ocean. But there are large areas which get almost no rain at all from the sea. They may get mists from the rivers, swamps, and lakes. In the wet season the rivers flood the land, and the largest irrigation system in the world within the limits of a single river system is in the Punjab of India and Pakistan. Yet some places are getting drier and drier. More water is blown out of these areas than is blown in.

POVERTY

The output of the fertile lands in South Asia is enormous, but the population is often so dense that the people do not get enough to eat. Their farming methods and implements are often very primitive. Most of the people use the same methods and the same implements their ancestors used thousands of years ago. There are few great tracts of land for expansion. Some of this huge area is far too dry. Some is far too cold. Some is too remote. The white towers of the mountains, the tawny wastes of sand, the flooded delta lands offer no welcome to the human race. Too little of the land is good enough for habitation.

So the people suffer from poverty everywhere. Their lot is little better than that of the wretched bullocks they use in their paddies and wheat fields.

INDEPENDENCE

These are general comments on South Asia. When we begin to study the individual countries we find vast changes taking place. The most important change is the almost complete disappearance of imperialism and colonialism. The French and British colonies have been succeeded by self-governing nations, though a few are still ruled by constitutional monarchs. Syria became a republic in 1941. India and Pakistan became independent members of the British Commonwealth in 1947, Ceylon in 1948. Burma became a republic in 1948, Malaya an independent federation in 1944. Iraq revolted against King Faisal in 1959 and killed him. On September 16, 1963, the Federation of Malaysia was set up with British support to include Malaya, Singapore, Sarawak, and North Borneo, also called Sabah.

The winds of change have been blowing everywhere in South Asia. There has been fighting in Malaya, India, Iraq, and Syria. A new nationalism has sprung up, and over the mountains in mainland China a mighty new threat to nationalism has appeared in the form of communism. The cold war is reaching into these countries, with the Soviet Union, the Western Powers, and Communist China vying with each other to win the support of the new nations.

EMERGING PROBLEMS

With independence have come many other problems. The new government officials are not always competent. They are inexperienced, often greedy for power, sometimes corrupt. The people are impoverished, illiterate, wedded to old customs, caught in the old economy that is now decaying. The caste system of Hinduism still shackles the people. Ancient superstitions blind them. There is a lack of trained leadership and a frightful lack of capital to do all the many things that need to be done so quickly. Undernourishment and disease take a terrible toll each year.

PROGRESS

Yet every government in South Asia is trying to improve the lot of the people. Each of them is building new schools, new clinics and hospitals, new roads and railways, new dams and irrigation canals, new factories, mines, and oil wells. Progress is evident everywhere, but the way ahead is long, tortuous, and difficult.

SOUTH ASIA IS OUR CONCERN

What does this mean to us in America? The United States is the greatest Pacific power in the world. Its influence is spreading into every country we shall visit in our book. There is hardly a nation in this whole region that is not looking to America for help. More and more we are reaching out into this part of the world with financial assistance, with counsel, and with expert know-how.

The Far East has become for the United States the Near West. South Asia is as close to us as South America. The threat of communism to India gives us the same headache as the presence of communism in Cuba. South Asia is our concern. It is your concern.

2. THAILAND

LAND OF THE FREE

THE LAND OF THE FREE

The Star-Spangled Banner describes America as the "land of the free." Thailand thinks it has a far better right to this title than we have.

Thailand has been independent since 1350 A.D. It was the only nation in southeast Asia to stay free during the nineteenth century, when the French, the English, and the Dutch were scrambling for the power and prestige that many colonies would give them. For a time it was the only free country between Japan and Persia.

However, the courage of Thailand's soldiers was not the only reason that country was able to stay independent. Its rulers were wise enough to play one great power against another. It remained free chiefly because of its value as a buffer state.

EARLY HISTORY

The people of this country are very like the Chinese. They probably came from somewhere in central Asia. The Chinese did not have a very high opinion of them, however. In the sixth century B.C. one Chinese writer spoke about the "barbarians to the south of us." The Chinese called the country at that time *Sien*, and the nations to the east of it called it *Syam*. From these two words came the name by which the country was known for so long, *Siam*.

In the thirteenth and fourteenth centuries a strong kingdom grew up in the north of Siam. This gave way later to another strong kingdom in the south. The latter kingdom was concerned for the welfare of the common people. It passed laws which said how much land a man could have. Even the poorest peasant was allowed ten acres. And as the soil was rich and irrigated by many streams, the people of this state were probably the best fed people in all Asia at that time.

THE KING AND I

Modern Siam began with King Mongkut in the middle of the nineteenth century. He had learned English from the missionaries, and he wanted his children to learn English too. So he hired an Englishwoman, Mrs. Anna Leonowens, to teach them. Many of you have seen the movie called *The King and I*, which tells the amusing experiences of this teacher at the king's court.

THREE HUNDRED AND SIXTY-TWO CHILDREN

King Mongkut's son was Chulalongkorn. He was probably the most important ruler in Siam's history. He had learned

English from Anna. It is said that he had 84 wives and 362 children. The kings of Siam at this time had so many children that something had to be done about them. So a system was invented by which the descendants of a king were gradually reduced in rank until a great-great-grandson of a king lost his title altogether.

THE LAND OF THE ELEPHANTS

There are so many elephants in this country that it has been called the "Land of the Elephants." Three kinds of elephants are found here: the wild ones, the sacred white elephants, and the work elephants, many of whom are employed to move heavy lumber in the teak forests. Teak is the most important of the woods found in this country.

King Mongkut wrote to Abraham Lincoln offering to send him many elephants "to roam through the jungles of America" and to provide beasts of burden for the people. The President replied that the United States lay in too high a latitude for elephants, and that "steam has been our best and most efficient agent of transportation."

RECENT HISTORY

In 1932 the government of the country was overthrown. The king was forced to abdicate, and later the boy prince, Ananda Mahidol, was called to the throne. He was only nine at the time, and eleven years later he was killed. The mystery of his violent death has never been solved. His brother, Phumiphon Aduldet, who was eighteen, succeeded him.

In 1939 the government decided not to use the old name of Siam any more. The official name became Muang Thai, which meant the land of the free. Westerners have called it Thailand ever since.

It was in that same year that the Second World War broke out in Europe. On December 7, 1941, Japan entered the war. She quickly overran all of southeast Asia. Thailand became an ally of Japan and declared war on the United States and Great Britain. It is doubtful that Thailand was really "the land of the free" at that time, though the Japanese never annexed the country, or treated it as a conquered state.

THE LOTUS

Thailand is in the middle of southeast Asia. It is bounded on the south by the Gulf of Siam, on the east and north by Cambodia and Laos, and on the west by Burma. It has an area of about 200,000 square miles and a population of twenty-eight million. To the west, north, and northeast there are mountains, and through the center of the country from north to south there are mountain ranges and valleys. A few of these mountains are about eight thousand feet high, but most of them are less than a mile high. The mountains become a rolling country and in the south they flatten out into a level plain.

The Mekong River forms the eastern boundary for a long distance. This is one of the great rivers of southeast Asia, twenty-five hundred miles long. The largest river in Thailand itself is the Menam, which flows into the Gulf of Siam. This serpentine river should really be called the Menam Chao Phraya, since Menam in the language of the country means *only river*.

One extraordinary geographical feature is the long sliver of land that runs down the eastern side of the Malay Peninsula for about 600 miles. For about half that distance Thailand shares the peninsula with Burma, the boundary between the

They often wear also pagodalike headdresses (called *pantiourets*) and long curved fingernails, which they attach to their own fingers. These fingers are very flexible and all the movements of the dancers are extremely graceful. Feeling is expressed by gestures, and no word is spoken. If a dancer passes her thumb and forefinger across her upper lip, as if to raise it, the gesture means a smile.

There are folk dances, courting dances (the boys are girls), and many others. The dancers give scenes from the old epic tale of India, called the *Ramayana*, or the "glory of Rama."

The dancers are accompanied by an orchestra, which consists of drums, lovely toned xylophones with bamboo keys, and a kind of flute.

In recent years other dances have become popular. One of them is *ram wong*, a folk dance from the northeast, when men and women dance round and round, though the men never touch the women. Other modern dances from the west are also catching on with the young people.

KITE FIGHTING

In front of the Grand Palace there is a big parade ground called the *Phramane*. Every year the March and April winds bring out the kites. This is a sport for grown-ups as well as children. The field is divided in the middle by a rope barrier. On the side away from the wind, little female kites are flown. On the other side are the big male kites, about twelve feet long and shaped like birds. The female kites try to bring down the male kites in their half of the field. The male kites also try to capture the female kites and haul them back to their half of the field. The male kites have bamboo barbs on the cord near the kite to entangle the small kites. Still the

two countries being a range of mountains in the center of the peninsula.

On the map Thailand looks very much like a big lotus flower growing on a long stem.

THE PEOPLE AND HOW THEY LIVE

The people, as we have said, are closely related to the Chinese, and the language is made up of single-syllable words like that of the Chinese. But there are many Chinese in the land who have come into it in recent years. About eight hundred thousand are still Chinese citizens, and about two million have some Chinese blood. Most of the retail merchants are Chinese, and most of the importing and exporting are in Chinese hands.

The great majority of the people are farmers, however. The farms average about four acres each. The methods used are often very primitive: the plowing is shallow, the weeding is careless, and little manure is used. At harvest time one rice stalk at a time is cut by hand with a knife. At the end of a day a man may carry home one or two loads on his back. That represents a day's work. The threshing is done by hand. The people use water buffaloes and bullocks.

Rice is the principal crop and there are sprawling rice lands everywhere. Ninety-five per cent of the planted land grows rice. Rice supports nine-tenths of the people.

However, the people also grow spices, coconuts, and rubber. They cut a great deal of teak, and they mine considerable quantities of tin.

Fuel is scarce, and rice husks are burned even in the power houses of the capital.

The low land is often flooded and most of the rural houses

are built on poles. They look like long-legged water spiders. The roofs are thatched, though tiles and corrugated iron are taking the place of thatch in the cities.

THE VENICE OF THE ORIENT

The capital of Thailand is Bangkok, a city of two million people. The Thai name is *Krung Thep*, which means the "metropolis of the gods." It's so full of canals that people have said that it's just like Venice or Amsterdam. The plain in southern Thailand is only about four inches above sea level, so whenever new roads had to be built in the city, the earth on the side was excavated to make an embankment for the road. Thus, every new road meant a new canal. Today some of these canals are being filled in to widen the roads.

The city, however, has many broad avenues now, spacious hotels, fine public buildings, and other structures. And the suburbs are reaching out into the countryside to cover the old rice paddies.

The canals that still run everywhere through Bangkok are lined with floating houses and stores. They are the streets, the front yards of the houses, the sewers, the bath houses. They are also the markets, where paddling peddlers sell vegetables, fruits, fish, and prepared meals from their boats.

On the streets themselves there are *samlors* (three-wheeled vehicles) rushing about everywhere. The samlor is a little taxi, in which the driver sits over the engine on a separate front seat. In back there is room for two passengers.

Not long ago there were no roads leading out of Bangkok at all. The only roads in the country outside the capital led to railway stations. Now there are both main roads and railways extending into every part of the land. During the war

the Japanese built a railway to Burma. They forced prisoners of war to work on it. The story of the construction is a terrible tale of suffering. One hundred thousand workers died.

MOSLEMS AND BUDDHISTS

In the southern part of the Malay Peninsula the people are mainly Moslems, but nearly everywhere else they are Buddhists. One-third of all the 150 million Buddhists in the world live in Thailand, Cambodia, Laos, and Burma. In the first three of these countries Buddhism is the state religion. In Thailand alone there are 165,000 monks and 20,000 monasteries. Every morning there is a golden parade of monks, clad in their deep yellow robes, often sheltering their shaven heads from the hot sun under big black umbrellas, and bearing their begging bowls, into which the people place food for the one meal a day they are allowed to eat.

Buddhists believe that all life is full of pain, and that by an eightfold path the devout Buddhist can escape from it and win salvation and peace in Nirvana. The eightfold path means right speech, right conduct, right living, right meditation, right belief, and so forth. Buddhism is a gentle religion, a religion of self-sacrifice, of pity for all living things. Its lovely temples and little shrines are to be found all through southeast Asia and particularly in Bangkok where the temples rise by the hundreds like bright, proud garden flowers.

CLASSICAL DANCING

Thailand is very fond of classical dancing. This is a very difficult art and it takes many years to become perfect in it. Both the male and the female parts are played by girls. They wear very rich, embroidered costumes, studded with gold

small kites sometimes bring down the big ones. When a kite is captured a ransom has to be paid for it. Thousands of people come out to watch the kite fights.

The first of the young people to greet us in this book is a lovely girl, Tipawan Thamthiangsat, who plans to be a classical dancer. She has been studying for four years now, and she has eleven more years of instruction.

Our second young person is a boy from the border of Laos in the north. He was abandoned by his parents and is now trying to learn the tailor's trade.

I'M A CLASSICAL DANCER

by Tipawan Thamthiangsat

THE SCHOOL OF DRAMATIC ARTS

Four years ago I applied for admission to the School of Dramatic Arts in Bangkok. This is under the government Department of Fine Arts and directed by the Minister of Education. They studied my academic record, my figure, my face, and my promise as a dancer. Finally I had to pass a special examination. I thought I was very lucky when they admitted me. My family and my friends were quite excited about it.

So I've been studying here for four years and it will be eleven more years before I finish my instruction. Then I'll be twenty-five.

There are three different departments in the school: Thai instruments, Thai dancing, and Thai singing. During the first six years I shall be in the elementary class and I can only take one of these. I chose dancing. After that I can choose one other subject, and I will take instruments.

There are nine hundred students in my school, more girls

than boys. About eighty of the girls live at the school, which is on the grounds of an old palace. There is a big Buddhist temple here. The school is building a new dormitory now, but the ground floor will be used for dancing.

WHEN I WAS SMALL

I was born in Bangkok fourteen years ago. This was the year 2492 in the Buddhist Era. I first went to a government primary school where I stayed for four years. I studied Thai, arithmetic, history, and geography. Then I left for my present school.

I was interested in dancing as far back as I can remember. I loved to dramatize stories I had heard, and I used to take part in the folk dancing in my neighborhood. I didn't play many outdoor games, for my people think that is not ladylike. But I did like to race.

MY HOME

My father is employed by the Thai Tobacco Company, and my mother is at home all the time. There are seven of us children, six girls and one boy. The oldest is a girl of sixteen. The youngest is a boy of seven. I'm the third oldest.

We live in the city in a two-story wooden house, on a narrow lane that leads off a main road. There is one big room on the ground floor and two rooms upstairs. We have no heat, but we do have electric light and running water. There are a kitchen and a bathroom outside.

MY DAILY PROGRAM

I get up at six, clean my room, sweep the floors, and help in the kitchen. I wash and iron my own clothes on the weekends. If I get up too late, I may have my breakfast in school, for we have a canteen there.

I arrive in school at eight fifteen after about an hour's ride in the bus, and from eight fifteen to eleven thirty I have mostly academic studies, though I do have singing and solfeggio. Of my academic subjects I like algebra the best.

From eleven thirty to twelve thirty is our lunch time. I often buy my lunch, though I could bring it if I wanted to. I usually eat Thai food.

The afternoon session is from twelve thirty to four thirty. For two hours I study the theory of dancing and for the next two hours I practice dancing.

At school I wear a uniform, a white blouse with a blue skirt and a blue bow tie. If we are in mourning we put on a black skirt. And we always wear black shoes. The initials of the school are worn on the right side of the blouse, with the number of the student. My number is 2119.

At four thirty I go home. I take a bath and if I have homework I do it then. If not, I usually take care of the little ones in the family. I have dinner at seven: rice, curry, vegetables, fish or meat. Sometimes I have sweets and fruit and I drink water. After that I may do some more homework or I may watch television. I go to bed at eight.

WORK AND PLAY OUTSIDE THE SCHOOL

My father doesn't have a car and I haven't any bicycle, so I spend the weekends at home. I mend clothes, wash and iron, and watch television. My father goes out with his friends and my mother takes care of the children and takes time for walks. On Sunday, Mother often makes something nice to eat and I can invite my friends.

My grandmother, who comes from Laos, lives with us. She has a place in the country and sometimes I go there with her during vacations. But often we hire a bungalow on the sea-shore at different beaches. Then I swim a great deal, roam around, and gather shellfish.

MY RELIGION

I'm a Buddhist like most of the Thai people, but we don't go to the temple regularly the way some Christians go to church. Usually we go only on special occasions. When I go it is often with my grandmother. However, we have a feast day every week which is called *Wan Phra*. On this day we don't kill any animals for food. In the morning we set food out on a table in front of the house for the priests. Then we go to the temple to pray. The door of the main temple is open and the priest gives a special sermon. We burn joss sticks, and offer flowers and fruit.

The feast in memory of Buddha's birth, enlightenment, and death is called *Visaka*. This, of course, is a very important day for us.

I COME FROM THE BORDER OF LAOS
by Phiboon Saskuan

THE BORDER OF LAOS

I was born about sixteen years ago in the year 2489 of the Buddhist Era (B.E. 2489). I don't know the exact date. The place was Ubol Rajdhani, which is up in the north near the border of Laos. It was one of the old capitals of Thailand. Until a year ago I spent all my life there.

There were many North Vietnamese in that region and they were all Communists. We never had any trouble with them, but when the Americans came, they all ran away across the border. I saw the American soldiers arrive and we all liked them very much. The men used to give candy to the children. Now some of the soldiers have been taken away, but the rest are still there.

MY PARENTS ABANDONED ME

My father and mother were tailors. We lived about two or three kilometers away from the center of the town. My house was a wooden house, one in a row, and very small. It had only one room in it, and this served as the kitchen and the tailor shop too. The toilet was outside.

My name in Thai is Phiboon Saskuan, and I have a Christian name, Paul. When I use that, it's my middle name. I have one younger sister who is blind in one eye.

My parents did not care anything about me, and did not have enough money to support me. But the Catholic bishop was very good to me. He put me in a school run by the sisters and paid the fee for me. I went to this school for six years, from the first elementary to the second grade. I studied Thai, history, geography, arithmetic, and a little English (very little). In school I wore a uniform just like all the other boys, white shirt and khaki shorts. At home I just wore shorts, and I went barefoot.

Outside my school I played football and *tacraw*. The latter is played with a hollow ball about five inches in diameter, which is made of cane. The object is to keep the ball in the air by hitting it with the shoulders, the head, the knees, the elbows, the heels, that is, with any part of the body except the hands.

I used to go fishing too; this was not for sport but to get something to eat. I fished from the banks of the streams and almost always could get enough fish for a meal or two.

My parents were Buddhists, but I was baptized as a Christian when I was very small. Finally my parents ran away to another province called Surindr, abandoning my sister and me, but the Bishop recommended me to the Don Bosco Technical School and Orphanage in Bangkok, and I came here a year ago. My sister stayed with the nuns in Ubol Rajdhani. She has been there since she was very young.

Since my parents never loved me and don't want me now,

I'm going to change my name next year. I'm taking the name of *Vongspheemph*. *Vongs* is the name of the clan my people belong to and *Pheemph* means printer. However, I'm not going to be a printer; I'm studying the tailor's trade.

THE DON BOSCO SCHOOL

I was a rather wild boy when I first came to my present school in Bangkok. The first night I was here I ran away and slept in the fields. They found me and took me back, but then I refused to eat. Finally one of the fathers told me that if I didn't eat he'd beat me. So I ate.

Now I like the school very much. It's an orphanage as well as a technical school. It's run by the Salesian Fathers, and it's very new. Three years ago there were only rice paddies where the school stands. Now we have school rooms and workshops, dormitories and a dining hall. They have planted trees and flowers and built concrete tennis courts. Just now a beautiful, big church is going up, which will be used by the boys in the school and by the people in the vicinity.

At school they teach woodworking, carving, printing, tailoring, metalwork, auto repairing, and other trades. In the woodworking shop at present the boys are making a huge cross for the church. We take orders for printing, metalwork, and other things. So the school makes a little money toward its expenses. None of us has to pay any tuition, and this is the only school in all Thailand that takes boys without a fee.

The headquarters of the Salesian Fathers is in Zurich, Switzerland, and they specialize in youth education all over the world, particularly for poor boys. Some of the fathers come from Italy. The director, Father Comiero, comes from Venice.

MY WORK IN SCHOOL

I'm in standard four now and taking Thai, English, math, history, geography, and science. But most of the day I spend learning my trade, which is the most important thing for a boy like me to do. My uniform at school consists of a white shirt, with D.B. (for Don Bosco) on it in red, blue shorts, and black shoes.

We have to get up at five fifty and we have twenty minutes for cleaning up. Then we go to mass and study for forty-five minutes before we have our breakfast. Our breakfast is rice, vegetables, sometimes sweets, with water to drink. We often have meat too.

From eight forty-five to twelve noon I'm in the tailoring shop. We mend clothes and make uniforms for the boys. We also get some orders from outside. After the morning's work we have lunch, which is like our breakfast but more abundant.

Burmans seldom use ordinary salt on the table. They put a layer of fish in a dish, cover it with salt, and let it stand. Then they squeeze it out and use the liquid for salt. The liquid, of course, has a fishy taste, but we like that.

At one o'clock we go outdoors to play for a while, and then we go to the study hall and rest for a half hour with our heads on our arms. A little snack follows: pineapples or bananas or some sweet. At five we take a bath, from five thirty to seven we are in class, and at seven we have a dinner which is like our lunch. Then we are allowed to play for a while. We have prayers at eight, go to the study hall for half an hour, and at eight forty-five we are in bed. Of course, we have night prayers before we go to bed.

The program for Saturday is just the same.

We have no work to do on Sunday. In the morning we have mass with a sermon. Then we may play for a while before we go to the study hall from eleven to twelve. After our noon meal we study again from one to two thirty or two forty-five. For the rest of the afternoon we are free. Some of us go to walk in groups. Some of us go to the market to buy things. The boys have to find their own spending money. For a time the bishop used to send me a little money but he has stopped doing that. So I buy some things at the market and sell them to the other boys. It's a kind of black market, for the school has a rule against this, but it's the only way I have to get a little money for myself.

Usually on Saturday evening at eight, but sometimes on Sunday, we have movies.

VACATIONS

After each term we have a vacation. The first two are for ten days each, the third is for thirty or forty days. I have nowhere to go, so I stay at the school.

I like music and I wish I could play a clarinet, but I don't have the money to buy one.

3. MALAYA

LAND OF THE RUBBER TREES

THE SOUTHERN TIP OF ASIA

If you travel south from Bangkok down the Malay Peninsula you will finally come to the most southerly point in Asia.
On the way you will pass through the Isthmus of Kra, which
is only seventeen miles wide and from a geographical point of
view the place where the peninsula really begins. This isthmus
is wholly within Thailand.

Some day a canal may be built across the isthmus. It would
save hundreds of miles in the sea voyage around South Asia.
From this narrow place Thailand stretches down another four
hundred miles southeast. Then you come to Malaya, which
continues in the same direction for 325 miles more.

The western coast of Malaya is covered with swamps. The
eastern coast is exposed to the northeast monsoons, which send
high waves dashing against the shore. These breakers wash
away the mud and leave white sand everywhere. There are
many islands off both shores.

RAIN FORESTS

The interior of the country is one vast rain forest, crossed by many rivers and small streams. The forest climbs the mountainous backbone of the country, which is nearer to the east coast than to the west. On top of the granite heights, but covered with red topsoil, there are enormous deposits of almost pure tin; the world's richest source of this metal is here.

It is not difficult to walk through the rain forest. Most of the trees are about 125 feet high but some of the giants tower more than 200 feet above the forest floor. As little sunlight penetrates to the ground, there is no dense growth of underbrush or small trees to make walking difficult.

Where the streams break through the forest, the sun enters and along the banks you find thick, sometimes almost impenetrable jungle.

ELEPHANTS, TIGERS, AND COMPANY

The Malayans say they have more tigers in their land than any other people in the world. You can hear them moan in the forest sometimes. There are also elephants, which do a great deal of damage to the banana plantations, for they love this fruit. They like to rub their backs against the telephone poles and often knock them down. The small houses of the natives are very frail and sometimes the people build barbed wire enclosures to keep the elephants off. But the trumpeting herds have been known to rush through a village and leave nothing but ruins behind. The elephant tracks are frequently used as trails for the people, since there are few roads in the interior.

There are many reptiles in the land, particularly near the

streams. The crocodiles are there, lurking in the rivers. Some places are alive with snakes. These include the King Cobra, the largest of all the poisonous serpents in the world. Sometimes he is eighteen feet long, and he can strike half his length with his deadly fangs.

You might meet the barking deer, or the little *plandok*, the smallest deer in the world. He weighs about three pounds and is about seven inches high at the shoulders. The flying fox is here, too. He's the largest bat in the world. There are many monkeys. There are fish that actually climb trees, and many strange birds, few of which have any real song. One bird, the *serendit,* sleeps upside down.

One of the most troublesome of all the jungle creatures is the leech. It's about the size and shape of a match and it travels along like a measuring worm. It can get into the eyelets of your shoes and suck the blood through your socks without your knowing it. But it prefers to climb up your clothing until it reaches your neck and takes its meal there. You can't feel its bite and when it is gorged with blood, and has become as big as a cigar, it drops down inside your clothes and takes a nap while it digests its food. The leech is not a pleasant companion.

THE PEOPLE

In this country of about 52,000 square miles there are over seven million people—Malays, Chinese, Indians, and others. The nation is very advanced. There is a good system of roads in the east and west, some very fine buildings in the cities, a balanced budget with no help from the outside, and a prosperous economy. Malaya has been called a paradise of high profits and low taxes.

Less than half the land is cultivated and the country is not self-sufficient in food. But it exports large quantities of tin and rubber. The rubber trees came originally from Brazil. The seeds were stolen and taken to Kew Gardens not far from London. From there the seedlings were sent to Malaya. The trees grow below a thousand feet on the hillsides and they like heavy rainfall. In 1920 Malaya produced 50 per cent of the world's rubber. In 1956, it is estimated that 90 per cent of it came from Southeast Asia. Now synthetic rubber is widely used, and this has forced the price down.

The third crop in Malaya is the coconut. The tree begins to bear when it's about six years old and continues bearing for some sixty years. Each tree has from forty to sixty nuts. A great deal of rice is grown too, but rice takes so much work that the natives prefer to grow rubber. Finally there's the pineapple. Malaya's crop is next to Hawaii's in export value.

FOREIGN RULERS

The Arabs, the Portuguese, the Dutch, and the British have ruled in Malaya. In 1403 the Arabs settled in Malacca, a place in the west on the Strait of Malacca. The Arabs were followers of the prophet Mohammed, and soon all the people in the southern peninsula were Moslems.

In the long decades that followed, the nation was often attacked by outsiders. The Bugis came from Borneo and other islands as far away as the Philippines. Some of their chiefs became sultans among the Malays. Siam often sent its armed forces in, and the Malay rulers sometimes had to pay tribute. It was a special kind of tribute, an ornamental plant with leaves of silver and flowers of gold. It was called *bunga mas*.

SIR STAMFORD RAFFLES

Sir Stamford Raffles was appointed the British agent to the Malay States in 1810. He established his headquarters on an island at the tip of the peninsula, called *Singa Pura*. This was Sanskrit for "lion city," and from these two words we get our modern word "Singapore." Raffles thought the Malays lazy and brought in thousands of Chinese to build up the country. He was a very able and far-seeing administrator.

The little swampy island of five thousand people that Raffles found, an island often attacked by pirates, is now a fine big city of 1.7 million people.

STRAITS SETTLEMENTS

Singapore and Malaya were governed before the Second World War as a single colony. They lay just east of the long Strait of Malacca. On the other side of the strait was the big Indonesian island of Sumatra. In addition to Singapore the Straits Settlements included the island of Penang, which lay at the northern end of the Strait of Malacca, just off the western shore of the Malay Peninsula; three other islands; and the mainland provinces of Wellesley and Malacca. The real name of Penang is George Town.

MALAYA

Malaya itself came to include the Straits Settlements—five Malay states, ruled by sultans and federated together, and five unfederated states, also ruled by sultans. Among the latter was Brunei, a protected sultanate on the big island of Borneo.

Because of its rubber and tin, Malaya was very important

to Britain. It was important also because Singapore was Britain's greatest naval base in Asia.

All this made Malaya very attractive to the Japanese during the Second World War. To everyone's amazement they captured Singapore easily by coming down through the peninsula and attacking the city from the poorly defended land side, rather than from the strongly fortified sea side.

After the defeat of Japan and its withdrawal from Malaya the Communists, who had become strong among the Chinese of Malaya, began to make trouble. For twelve years they carried on a baffling guerrilla war in the interior forests. They were never defeated by force of arms, but by 1951 they had been starved out.

INDEPENDENCE

In April, 1946, the British government established a union of nine native states. It took away much of their power from the native rulers, and set up a separate government for Singapore. The Malays did not like this, and the plan was abandoned. A temporary federation was then set up. Finally in 1957, Great Britain granted independence to Malaya and ceded to it the islands of Penang and Malacca. Malaya then became a constitutional monarchy in the British Commonwealth with a head of state and a prime minister, the only free nation in the Commonwealth besides Great Britain to have its own monarch. The following year Singapore also became a self-governing state within the Commonwealth.

SARAWAK AND BRUNEI

Besides Singapore and Malaya, Britain also had two colonies on the northern coast of Borneo. (Borneo ranks as the third

largest island in the world; only Greenland and New Guinea
are larger.)

One of these colonies was Sarawak, with an area of 50,000
square miles and a population of about 745,000 people. The
other was Brunei, just north of Sarawak and very much
smaller, with 2,000 square miles and a population of 85,000.
But it had the important Seria oil fields, which produce five
million tons of oil a year. These fields are the largest in the
British Commonwealth.

THE WHITE RAJAH

How these colonies came under British control is an interesting story. A British civil servant in India died and left his
large wealth to his son, James Brooke. The son wanted to
explore the island of Borneo, and bought a big yacht for the
purpose. At that time the Sultan of Borneo, who also ruled
Sarawak, was having a great deal of trouble. His people were
in revolt against him. Then in the interior, there was a tribe of
head-hunting aborigines called "Dyaks," a strange people who
lived in long houses which sometimes accommodated a hundred families and sailed in long boats made out of big trees.
These Dyaks were on the warpath with their blowguns and
poisoned arrows. Finally, to complete his troubles, pirates
were raiding the coasts.

So the Sultan offered to make Brooke the governor of
Sarawak if he would put down the revolt and drive off the
pirates. Brooke did so. Then in 1846 the Sultan ceded Sarawak
to Brooke, who became the White Rajah and ruled until his
son Charles took over. In 1946 the country became a British
colony.

Sarawak is a land of pepper vines. The ripe berries are

orange-colored. Black pepper comes from the dried berries. White pepper comes from berries whose skins have been soaked off.

MALAYSIA

There was another crown colony to the northeast of Brunei in Borneo. This was British North Borneo, or Sabah. There were about 30,000 square miles in this colony, and a population of about 460,000.

Since the day of imperialism had passed and many former colonies had won their freedom, Great Britain decided it was time to get rid of her last colonies in this region. After careful planning with the representatives of the different countries, she decided to organize a new Federation of Malaysia to include Malaya, Singapore, Sarawak, Brunei, and Sabah. The federation was to be set up on August 31, 1963, but the opposition of Indonesia and the Philippines delayed the fulfillment of the plan until September 15. At the last moment Brunei decided not to join. Malaysia has about 130,000 square miles and ten million people. The capital is Kuala Lumpur, the former capital of Malaya.

Indonesia has announced her determination to destroy Malaysia.

The young people who represent Malaya come from the two largest groups in the country. Mariati bt. Aziz is a lovely Malay girl from the capital city, Kuala Lumpur. Tan Poay Lim is a bright Chinese boy from Penang.

A MALAY GIRL IN KUALA LUMPUR
by Mariati bt. Aziz

THE CLOTHES WE WEAR IN MALAYA

There are three major groups of people in my country.
Here in Kuala Lumpur, where I live, you can usually tell
them apart not only by the color of their skin and the shape
of their faces but also by the clothes they wear, particularly
if they are women. The Chinese live mostly in the cities, for
they are very good merchants, and their women wear two
different kinds of clothes. Some of them wear the slender,
form-fitting, one-piece, sleeveless *cheongum;* it has a high stiff
collar, and its skirt falls below the knees in two panels, front
and back, and is slit up the sides. But most of the Chinese wear
the two-piece *samfu.* The top has a high collar and off-
shoulder sleeves and it fastens under the right arm, the bottom is just like pajamas.

The Malays are mostly farmers and when the women are
dressed up they wear a long *kaim*, or sarong, that falls from
the waist to the ankles and either a rather loose upper garment
that comes to the knees and is called a *baju kurong*, or a form-
fitting blouse with an open neck.

The Indians are mostly workers on the great rubber plantations, though they are also merchants in the cities. The Indian women wear long dresses that fall to the ground and a long scarf, called a *sari*, that is usually thrown over one shoulder.

Many of the Indian women have red or black spots in the middle of their foreheads. Sometimes this means that they are married, sometimes that they have been to the temple, and sometimes it's just a beauty spot. Often little children have a spot of red on their foreheads. Some Indians believe in the evil eye, and this spot is supposed to protect the children from it.

As I am a Malay girl, I usually wear Malay clothes. At school, however, I wear a uniform, which consists of a white blouse and a blue pinafore with straps over the shoulders. But even when I'm not in school, I sometimes wear western clothes.

OUR NAMES

My name is Mariati bt. Aziz. The *bt.* stands for *binti*, which means "daughter of." My father, or *bapa*, is called Abdul Aziz bin Abu Hassan. The *bin* means the son of. He was born in Kuala Lumpur, but in 1961 he spent four months in America. The United States Information Service gave him a scholarship to study television, and he visited Washington, Los Angeles, and places in between observing the operation of TV stations. He also spent some time with the British Broadcasting Company in London. He is now in charge of program operations in the government department of broadcasting, which has a number of stations throughout Malaya.

My mother, or *amak*, was born in a village about ten miles

from Kuala Lumpur. She went to England in 1958 and spent three and a half years there studying English and journalism. On the way back she traveled for five months in many parts of the States. She now writes a column twice a week for a Malayan newspaper. She has always been active in politics, and in 1962 she was appointed a senator. She is the first and only woman in the senate of my country.

I have three brothers. Shairudin bin Abdul Aziz is fifteen. He wants to be an engineer. Astaman bin Abdul Aziz is nine, and Zahrim is one and a half. I was born here in Kuala Lumpur thirteen years ago, but not in the house where I now live.

THE MALAY AREAS

Although the three groups of people in Malaya get along together very happily, each group has its own areas where it must live. So we live in a Malay area. Bapa built our house, which is very large and airy. In fact it is too large for us, and Bapa now rents six of the rooms. The windows are not screened and so we sleep under mosquito nets. However, there is very little malaria in the country. We have electricity, running water, and every other convenience.

KINDERGARTEN AND LATER SCHOOLS

I don't remember very much about my early life, except that I was always hitting my older brother with a stick. But he was a tease too. The kindergarten I first went to at four years was a private school, and my father took me there each day on his bicycle. After a year there I went to a Malayan school for two years, and then I entered the school where I have been ever since. This is a Catholic school, attached to the Convent of the Holy Infant Jesus. There's a church there by the same name. I've been going to this school for seven years, and I'm now in form one. This follows the younger classes which run from standard one to six. Some of my teachers are nuns and some are lay teachers.

I'm studying the Malay language, English, math (arithmetic and algebra), history, geography, and general science. We have sports, too, and I play badminton; but I'm not on any school team.

I'd like to be a lawyer, and to do that I must go on through form five, lower and upper six, and then to the University of Malaya. There is a law school connected with the university.

MY DAILY ROUTINE

I get up at six and have a breakfast of bread and butter, eggs and tea. School begins at seven twenty, and I travel there on a bus. The ticket costs five cents (about a cent and a half in United States currency). In the middle of the morning we have a fifteen-minute break, when I have noodles or a sandwich to eat and something cold to drink. School ends for the day at one fifty.

The main dish for lunch and dinner at home is rice with either fish or meat. In the afternoon I do some homework, help with the housework, and play badminton on a court in the neighborhood. I always play with my brother, never with other boys and girls. As a matter of fact there are not many other girls living in our neighborhood, and Moslem girls like myself don't have the freedom that American girls seem to have. However, I don't mind this and I have lots of good times with my own family.

In the evening I have more homework to do, and sometimes

I play snakes and ladders with my brother. This is something like parcheesi. I go to bed about nine thirty.

WEEKENDS AND VACATIONS

We have no school on Saturday and Sunday. On Saturday I do a good deal of work about the house, cleaning and washing. On Sunday the family often goes off for a picnic together. It's about thirty miles to the shore, and we often go there. About fifty miles away is a park called Templer Park, where there are lovely forests, waterfalls, and streams. We enjoy this park very much.

Our long vacation is from December 1 to the middle of January. Then I often go to visit friends in other Malayan cities. Sometimes I go to Penang; sometimes I go to Singapore. But I don't like Singapore very much.

I have a *baisikal*, and I think you can guess what this Malay word means. But I never go with other young people on picnics or other kinds of outings. I do dance a little, and I can do the folk dances of my people. I want to take up the piano, but I haven't begun yet.

THE MOSLEM RELIGION

In school there is always religious instruction and we Moslems get instruction in our own faith. In my country the women seldom go to the mosque. They get special teaching outside. Our most important religious festival is *Ramadan*, when we fast from dawn to sunset for a whole month. In the evening we have a meal and we can have another before daybreak, if we wish. At the end of Ramadan come two or three days of feasting, exchanging gifts, and visiting friends; this is called *Hari Raya Aidelfitri.* A little later there is another special celebration for those who have made the pilgrimage to Mecca.

MY LANGUAGES

I speak English and Malayan. The latter is somewhat different from the language spoken in Indonesia, but there is also much in common between the two tongues. We both say *Selamat pagi* for "good morning," *Selamat tinggal* for "goodby," and *Selamat datang* for "welcome."

A CHINESE BOY IN PENANG
by Tan Poay Lim

I BELONG TO THE HOKHIEN CLAN

Most of the Chinese in Malaya come from South China and belong to the Hokhien clan. That's the clan my family belongs to, and we all speak Hokhien at home. But I can speak Cantonese also, which is the most important language in southern China, and Mandarin, which is the official language for the whole country. Then, because my family has always lived in Malaya, I speak Malayan, and at school I have always been taught in English. So there are five languages that I speak.

AHPA AND AHMA

My father is Tan Chye Soon. Tan is our family name. He was born in the Province Wellesley, which is on the mainland opposite the island of Penang. He is now the cashier for a company which has just started to mine for tin in the northern part of the state of Perak, which runs up to Thailand in the center of the Malay Peninsula. His headquarters are in George

Town, which is usually called Penang, on an island in the Strait of Malacca. Twice a month he drives in his car to the mine to pay the workers. The tin is found in grains in the earth, and when the earth is washed the tin settles to the bottom.

I call my father *Ahpa*, which is the Hokhien word for father, and my mother I call *Ahma*. My mother was also born in Province Wellesley.

I have four brothers. The oldest is Tang Ham, who is now twenty-two. He has been studying pure chemistry for a year at the University of Perth in southwest Australia on a scholarship he received under the Colombo Plan. Now he has gone to the University of Sydney on another scholarship which has been granted to him by the Shell Oil Company. He will study chemical engineering there.

Next comes my brother Tang Keat, who is eighteen. He's an engineer on a British merchant ship that sails mostly around the Malay Peninsula; but he has been as far away as Hong Kong.

Tang Lok comes next. He's sixteen and he's studying at the technical school in Ipoh. He wants to be an electrical engineer.

I'm fifteen and then I have a younger brother, who is four.

MY CHILDHOOD

I was born in Penang and I still live in the same house. It's a small brick house with two rooms, a kitchen, and a bath. The windows are screened and it has all the conveniences.

I did not go to school until I was eight, so I had lots of time to play when I was a small boy. I used to spin tops with other boys, and each of us tried to knock the other tops out of the ring. I used to like to fly kites also, and February was kite-flying time. The kites were usually diamond-shaped and the frames were bamboo. We used ordinary string, but we used to make the string very hard and sharp by putting glue on it and hammering it. Then we used to try to cut each other's kites down by drawing the string across the strings of the other kites. I lost a lot of my kites, but I got a good many of the others too. Another game we played was marbles. Most of the boys I played with in those days have scattered now.

MY SCHOOLING

The first school I went to was the Wellesley Primary School, which was about three or four miles away from my home. I had to go every day in a taxi and I was there for two years. Then I went to another primary school for four years. This was the Francis Light School which was about two miles away from my house. I rode the bus to this school. Captain Francis Light was the man who took possession of the island of Penang for the British in 1786.

After that I came to my present school, which is the Penang Free School. This is the oldest school in all Malaya. It was founded in 1816, and the constitution says its purpose was "to provide for the education of such children as would otherwise be brought up in idleness and consequent vice and without any means of obtaining instruction either in useful learning or in any manual employment." The word "free" never meant that there was no charge for our schooling. Those who could paid one Malay dollar a month, and the old East India Company helped with the expenses. There are many public and grammar schools in England that are called "free," and that was where my school got its name. It's one of the best schools in all Malaya.

During the war, when the Japanese were here, the school was closed and the Japanese robbed it of almost everything it had. Only a few pieces of furniture remained when the Japanese had gone. They took all the books, all the equipment, and all the apparatus.

MY DAILY PROGRAM

I've been in this school for three years now and I'm in form three. I'm studying geography, history (Malay and European), Malayan, which we now call the national language, English, math, art, and physical education. Soon we are going to study about the United States. We have gymnastics and sports. The school is divided into five "houses." Teams from each house play the teams from the other houses. Our sports are rugby, soccer, cricket, hockey, and badminton. Last year I was on the cricket and rugby teams for my house.

There is a hostel at the school for about fifty boys who live far away, but the rest of us live at home. I come to school every day on my bicycle. It takes me about five or ten minutes.

I'm up in the morning at six forty-five, but I don't eat breakfast at home. Very few of the boys do, because there is a canteen at school where we can get good meals during the morning break from eleven to eleven thirty. The classes begin at seven forty and on three days in the week they end at one thirty. On the other days they end a little earlier.

Unless there is some special activity, I go home immediately after school. Then I eat a big meal, a Chinese kind of meal. I have a big plate of rice and on the rice bits of fish, meat, and vegetables that I choose from other dishes placed in the center of the table. We have fruits often, and I drink tea, coffee, and water. I like water best. After this I rest for half an hour. I may go back to school in the afternoon for school games, or I may go swimming. There's a good pool at a swimming club near by. I have homework to do also, both in the afternoon and the evening. Our dinner at seven is like the midday meal. Sometimes I play monopoly and scrabble. I'm in bed by ten o'clock.

I like all my school subjects, and I don't know yet what I want to do later. However, I do hope to go on to the university.

Our school uniform is usually all white. Younger boys such as myself wear shorts; older boys wear trousers. For special occasions we have a blue jacket with the seal of the school on the left breast pocket.

OTHER ACTIVITIES

On Saturday and Sunday we have no school. Then I help around the house, do some marketing for Ahma, and play games with the other boys in the neighborhood. Sometimes the family goes on a picnic, and sometimes I go for an outing with the other boys. We go to the beaches, and we organize hikes up the mountains and to the other side of the island.

During the three school vacations I go camping on the shore sometimes, or I visit friends in other places. I have friends in Ipoh and at Bukit Metajam in Province Wellesley. Once I went to the tin mine with my father. I can dance and play the harmonica, and I sometimes go to the movies. When I go to the beach with my family, I sometimes go fishing all night. What I get depends upon my luck.

SEA SCOUTS

I'm very enthusiastic about my Sea Scouts. There are four troops in Malaya and ours is called Eight George Town South. There are about fifty boys in the troop and they are organized into five patrols with a scoutmaster in charge of the whole program. We have Senior Sea Scouts, but the younger boys are just called "Sea Scouts." An Australian organization gave us a small boat, which is only about ten feet long; but it has an outboard motor and we have a lot of fun with it. The patrols take turns in using the boat, and we always go out with the scoutmaster. When we take the boat out during vacations, we may stay away for four days, camping somewhere in tents on the island. We learn to run the motor, we study sailing and navigation, knots, and other things.

Once when the motor wouldn't work we were out for five hours. We had to use the thwarts to paddle the boat back. We hope to get money for sails soon.

I'm a Buddhist, and there are about two hundred temples on the island of Penang. I go to one near our house, but I only go on special days to burn joss sticks and pray.

This is what my Hokhien dialect sounds like: *Wah seon bueh ki Bee kok*. This means "I should like to go to America."

4. BURMA

"THE HAPPIEST LAND IN ASIA"

ON THE ROAD TO MANDALAY

It wasn't very long ago when the only knowledge many of us had of Burma was contained in Rudyard Kipling's lines that went:

There's a Burma girl a-settin', and I know she thinks o' me; . . .
On the road to Mandalay,
Where the flyin'-fishes play,
An' the dawn comes up like thunder outer China 'crost the Bay!

It would be difficult to find a single sentence anywhere else which contains more inaccurate statements than this one. The important city of Mandalay, once the capital of Burma, is not on the sea at all. It's inland on the Irrawaddy River, and there are no flying fishes in this stream. Not only that, but there isn't a spot in all Burma where you can see the dawn come up "outer China 'crost the Bay."

THE BURMA ROAD

It was the opening of this famous road that made this country known throughout the world. The road was begun by the Chinese after the war with Japan broke out in 1937. It was finished in 1938. It became very important after the Japanese had occupied all the principal ports on the coast of China. The Chinese were still fighting the Japanese in the west, and it was necessary to get war supplies in to their armies. These supplies were landed at Rangoon, the present capital of Burma, and then shipped by railway to Lashio in Burma, where the road began. Then it climbed over the high mountains to China. Its construction was a miracle of engineering.

THE LEDO ROAD

During the Second World War, Japan occupied Burma and closed the Burma Road. Somehow the Allies still had to get supplies in to western China. So they built another road that started at Ledo in Indian Assam and from there went into Burma, following a centuries-old trail until it joined the earlier Burma Road. It was 478 miles long and one of the most difficult roads ever built anywhere. It was completed in 1944 after two years of very hard labor.

The men who built it had to hack their way through dense jungles of great hardwood trees, elephant grass, bamboo thickets, and hanging vines. They had to build bridges over ten big rivers and a hundred and fifty-five little streams. Finally the road joined the old Burma Road to climb over the Himalayas. One of the men who built this road said: "We froze in winter and sweat ourselves weak in summer. The monsoons were terrible. We were always wet and covered with festering sores from the bites of the jungle leeches. Malaria and typhus were as common as colds at home."

In addition to the supplies that went in on the ground, planes flew over what was called the "Hump." This was the most dangerous route in the world, with jagged peaks thrusting their snowcaps more than five miles into the skies, and passes more than three miles above sea level. The fliers had no beacons to mark the route. There were fogs and rains to obscure the land beneath them. The men said that some of the peaks were higher than Mount Everest, though this is very doubtful.

It isn't strange that the trucks traveling the Burma Road and the planes flying over the Hump made Burma known to the world.

THE GEOGRAPHY OF BURMA

Burma is bounded on the east by China, Laos, and Thailand. It comes to a point in the south at the Isthmus of Kra. In the west it is bounded by the Andaman Sea, the Bay of Bengal, Pakistan, and India. China lies to the north of it. Except where the sea washes the western coast, Burma is entirely ringed by mountains. It's not easy to get into the country unless you fly in or approach it by sea.

Burma is a big land of 260,000 square miles, almost the size of Texas. It is a tropical country, still largely underdeveloped. The great Irrawaddy River with its many tributaries and its enormous delta fills most of the interior, and forms a big central plain. Together with some coastal areas, this is where the people live and where most of the food is grown.

TWO REGIONS

There are two distinct regions in Burma. Lower Burma is the wet region of the Irrawaddy valley and the delta. This is the monsoon region. In the summer the prevailing winds are from the sea, and the rainfall is very heavy, over eighty inches a year. Here most of the paddy rice is grown. Upper Burma is the original home of the Burmese people. This part of the country gets much less rain and therefore crops that thrive in a rather dry climate grow here. There is also a semi-arid place in Central Burma.

Many primitive people live in Upper Burma. They still build suspension bridges with cane cables over the rivers. Often these bridges are built on the same principle as our suspension bridges over the Hudson or the Ohio Rivers. The ends of these strong vegetable ropes are fastened to trees or to wooden towers. The floors are sometimes wide, sometimes very narrow, just strips of bamboo laid at the bottom of a V-shaped tunnel. Once in a while a bridge may consist of a single rope with a wooden hoop that slides along the rope. A man crosses such a bridge by lying in the hoop and pulling himself along with his hands and his feet.

THE MONSOON FORESTS

The tropical forests are very dense in Burma. An American pilot flying over this forest crashed three minutes after take-off. The rescue party had to hack its way through the forest for a day and a half before they could reach him. The path they made was so rough that the injured pilot could not be carried over it, so a detachment of engineers was sent in. For two weeks they worked, carving out a tiny circular clearing in the midst of the tall trees where a helicopter could land, before they could take the pilot back to the hospital.

The world's principal source of teak is in this forest. There is a narrow belt on either side of the Irrawaddy, where about one-tenth of the trees are teaks. Teakwood is excellent for ship decks and for cabinet work. A full-grown tree is about six feet in circumference. Unfortunately the green wood is too heavy to float, so the tree is girdled three years before it is felled, in order that the wood may dry. Then it is floated down the streams, for that is the only way to get it out. Here is where the elephant and the buffalo are useful. They carry the logs to the rivers. No machine yet built can do this work.

Since it takes about four years for the trees to reach the market, a good deal of capital is required for this kind of lumbering.

"THE HAPPIEST LAND IN ASIA"

This is what Burma has been called. The British used to say that you could tell when you entered Burma by the smiles of the people. These friendly people are almost all farmers. Before the war Burma was the world's largest exporter of rice and teak. But the people also grow millet, rubber, ground nuts (peanuts), cotton, and tobacco.

One reason why Burma has been called the "happiest land in Asia" is that the country is not overcrowded, like its neighbor, East Pakistan. So there is food enough for everybody.

Another reason for happiness is that this is a Buddhist land, where there are no castes and no *purdah*, the system by which women are often hidden away from the eyes of the public.

RUBIES, SAPPHIRES, JADE

There are many mineral resources: iron, lead, silver, zinc, and wolfram. Lovely gems, like rubies and sapphires, are plentiful, and much of the jade sold in China and Hong Kong comes from Burma, which has been exporting it ever since the thirteenth century.

There are rich deposits of oil in the country. India, Burma, and Indonesia stand fourth today in the world's oil production. This region has enormous reserves and tomorrow it might well be first.

THE BRITISH IN BURMA

The British snatched Burma from the Manchu Empire in China in the eighteen-sixties. It then became a part of India; but in 1935 it was separated from the latter country.

Britain developed the resources of the land. Ten million acres of swamp and jungle were brought under cultivation; the mineral and oil resources were developed. This, however, did not benefit the mass of the people very much, since much of the work was done by Indian laborers, and all the large enterprises and most of the small ones were owned by the British or controlled by them. The people were gradually saddled with debt. They were poor and restless. They could no longer be described as "the happiest people in Asia."

FREEDOM

The Japanese occupied the country during the war and set up a puppet government there. After the Japanese withdrew and the British returned, the people demanded their freedom. On January 4, 1948, Burma became an independent country, but not a member of the British Commonwealth.

Since the war there have been many difficult days. Communism has been very troublesome; the need for land reform, education, and industrialization has brought many problems. These later years have been years of discontent and instability.

Most Burmese boys spend some time in a Buddhist monastery, and Khin Maung Win tells us of his life there. May May Kyaing was born way up in northeast Burma, near the Irrawaddy River and not far from the Chinese border. She tells us many interesting things about the life of a Burmese girl.

I WAS A NOVICE IN
A BUDDHIST MONASTERY
by Khin Maung Win

LIFE AT A BUDDHIST PAGODA

A Buddhist priest is called a *Djongyi* here. His head is shaved and he wears a deep yellow robe, which is wrapped around his body in such a way that the right shoulder is left bare. The priests have very strict rules. They live at the pagodas, but the only food they have is what they beg every day. They are not allowed to touch money and they cannot accept anything directly from a woman. A gift from a woman must be made through a man, or placed on the ground or a table. Food, of course, can be emptied into the begging bowl the monks carry.

A monk is only allowed to have eight different things: three pieces of cloth for his robes, a begging bowl, a mat, a blade, a needle, and a water strainer. He may also have articles that are needed for his religious life: religious books, candles, matches, brooms, and spittoons.

Sometimes on birthdays people invite the monks to their homes for a grand meal. Then they may receive as gifts the things they are allowed to have. Spittoons are considered the nicest presents. They are often made of white enamel with a red band around the edge.

A priest is always addressed as *Paya*, which means "Lord." The priest calls the layman *daga*, which means giver.

I BECOME A NOVICE

It is expected that every Burmese boy will become a novice at a pagoda for at least a short time. When I was eleven I went to a monastery near my home for a week. My head was shaved and I put on the yellow robe. Every day I got up at five thirty. My parents used to bring me some breakfast in the morning, but that was a special privilege that the novices had. Then I studied the scriptures and had prayers until ten. The head monk taught us. After that I went out begging with a black bowl. A Buddhist gains merit by giving to the monks, so I had no trouble filling my bowl. Back at the monastery we all shared alike. We had good food to eat, for the people were very generous.

After this meal in the late morning no more food is eaten until the next day, though we can have cold drinks. In the afternoon I studied the sacred books and prayed with my prayer beads. The older monks spent much time in meditation but the boys were not expected to do this.

The boys helped the monks in other ways. We swept the floors and the grounds, for everyone went barefoot. We drew water for drinking and for the baths of the older monks. We waited on the monks at meal time.

It was a good life. I liked it very much.

I WAS BORN AT NATTALIN

Nattalin is in the Tharawaddy District, about a hundred and forty miles from Rangoon, a town of about twenty thousand people. But I only lived there for two years and I don't remember anything about it. My father is an engineer working for the government. I have a mother, a sister of twelve, and two brothers of eleven and seven. I am fifteen.

My house in Rangoon, where we now live, is a bungalow. Here in Burma a bungalow always has two stories. A house with one floor only is called a cottage. The first floor of our house is of brick and the second floor is of wood. We have about ten rooms.

A METHODIST SCHOOL

I started my schooling at the Methodist High School when I was five. My family thinks this is the best school in the vicinity. I've been there ever since and now I'm in standard seven, studying Burmese, English, mathematics, history, geography, general science, and morals. Until last year we had school football, but this year we have no sports. I am very fond of math and I want to go on to the university to study accounting. My family has always been an educated family. My grandfather was headmaster of the biggest high school in the city.

When I go to school, I have to take off my comfortable *longyi* (a cloth tied about the waist which falls to the ankles) and put on a uniform. This consists of white shirt and trousers and a maroon tie. We wear no cap and no school emblem. We can wear any kind of belt or shoes we wish.

THE DAILY ROUTINE

I rise at six and breakfast on eggs, bread, coffee, and sometimes fruit. School begins at eight and my father drives me in his car. During the morning break I eat *mohinga*, which is a pasta dish like spaghetti, or *khaukswe*, which is made of Chinese noodles and is a specialty of this province.

School is out at one thirty and I go home on the bus. After a hearty meal I study for an hour, play tennis for two hours on a court near my home, and then take a bath. In the evening I study for another hour, listen to the radio, and go to bed at nine.

WEEKENDS AND VACATIONS

We have no school on the weekends. On Saturday nights I usually go to the movies. The family often goes on a picnic in the car. There is a nice lake about ten miles away called Hlawga Lake. From this lake Rangoon draws some of its drinking water, so we cannot swim, or fish, or go boating. But we can go to the pagoda there and enjoy a nice picnic lunch beside the lake. There are other places where I can swim in Rangoon.

Our long vacation comes in March and April, and all the family except my father, who can't get away from his work, goes back to Nattalin, where my grandparents, as well as uncles, aunts, and cousins, still live. All Burmese families think that the family ties are very important and that all children should know the old customs. So at Nattalin we never walk into the house with our shoes on, and we never eat at the table until the food has been placed in grandfather's plate.

BURMESE FESTIVALS

During the long vacation, usually on April 13th, there occurs the New Year's Festival. It's called *Thingyan* and it lasts for three or four days. This is the time when the spirit-king, the *Tha-gya Min,* comes back to visit the world of men. There is both fasting and feasting, meditation and prayer. But for the children the best fun is the water squirting. Big tubs of water are set out, and the children get pistons so that they can squirt water on everyone in the house. The children under eight are stripped naked and after they have soaked all the people indoors they run out into the streets to soak all the passers-by.

There's a Rice Harvest Festival in October, called *Tabodwe.* Then there's a beautiful Lantern Festival in October, called *Thadingyut,* when many thousands of lanterns are strung all over the city. We also shoot off firecrackers at that festival.

The big Buddhist festival is in July. It celebrates the birth, the enlightenment, and the death of Buddha. It also marks the beginning of the Buddhist lent. Fasting during lent is not compulsory for us.

THE SHWE DAGON PAGODA

Since we are all Buddhists we often go to the pagodas, and the greatest of them all is the Shwe Dagon Pagoda. *Shwe* means gold, and *Dagon* is the old name for Rangoon. This is said to be the highest Buddhist structure in the whole world. It stands on the top of a hill, and it's about 360 feet high. The huge central spire is covered with gold leaf, and at the tip of it there are many hundreds of little gold and silver bells and jewels worth a half million dollars.

When we visit the pagoda we make offerings of money, candles, incense, paper and real flowers, and at times even gold leaf.

I WAS BORN IN UPPER BURMA
by May May Kyaing

LONGYIS AND AINGYIS

Everyone in Burma wears *longyis* and *aingyis*, even most of the children. The longyi is a piece of cloth about four or five feet long which is wrapped around the waist and falls down to the ankles. The men tie it in front in a knot. The women fasten it over the right hip. But the men and women never wear the same pattern of fabric. The men use checks and plaids and stripes, mainly of gray, blue, and brown. The women usually have gay, flowered patterns of bright colors. Sometimes their longyis are made of silk.

The men wear a shirt above the longyi, just like an American shirt. The women wear a thin, white jacket, which is called an aingyi. This may have short or long sleeves, and it fastens at the neck and over the right side.

WEAR FOR THE ARMS

Burma is a jewel country. We don't find diamonds in Burma, but we have beautiful sapphires, and jade, and rubies.

The rubies are famous, and vary in color from a deep red and purple to a lovely pale rose. The Burmese women wear a great deal of jewelry, especially when they are dressed up. This is not thought to be showing off. Jewelry is just another piece of clothing in my country. We call jewels "wear for the arms," or the neck, and so on. Sometimes even the buttons that fasten the aingyi at the side have big jewels in them, but for ordinary wear, they are gold or gilt.

SCHOOL UNIFORM

At school I have to wear a uniform. This is a white blouse partly covered with a blue pinafore, a black belt, and shoes and white socks. I wear my hair in two long braids, as most girls do.

A TOWN ON THE IRRAWADDY RIVER

I was born in a town called Katha fifteen years ago. This town is in Upper Burma on the Irrawaddy River, not far from Bhamo, where my father was born, and not far from the big city of Mandalay. My mother, Daw Khin Htwe, was born in Katha too; but I have only vague memories of it, for I only stayed there until I was four.

Then we moved to Maymo, a town in the Shan States in the middle of Burma. My father is an officer in the army, and he had to go there for military training. The people of the Shan States belong to a minority group called *Shans*. There used to be several small Shan States, but now they are all grouped into a single state. My own people belong to the majority group, the Burmans.

At the end of six months there my father was transferred to a small city named Toungoo, where we lived in a house at a military camp just outside the city. I was there for two years, and it was then that I began to go to school. My father sent me to St. Joseph's Convent School, because that was the best school in the city.

My father's name is Aung Kyaing. For a long time the Burmans had no family names, but now they do. Our family name is Kyaing.

NURSERY RHYMES

I don't remember much about my early life. I played as other children do, and I did the things they do. We had nursery rhymes that I liked to say over and over again. There is one about a greedy cat:

> Oh you big and short-tailed cat,
> Swallowing the lean
> And eating the fat.

There's another about an old man:

> Old man, so bent and gray,
> Do not die as yet, we pray.
> Till next December try to tarry
> And watch the actors play and marry.

And one about a frog too:

> From waters of Meiktila Lake
> Pick up a frog for me.
> Poor little frog,
> Eyes big agog,
> And body so thin and wee.

I'M THE OLDEST

I have three younger sisters. They are eleven, six, and four. They all call me "Elder Sister." I call each of them "Younger Sister." My father I call "Pe Pe," and my mother "May May." The latter is my name too. We are taught to call an official, a man of importance, or an old man "U." This is just a polite form of "Mister." "Daw" is the word we must use for a woman, but it doesn't mean a married woman.

WE MOVE TO RANGOON

We came to Rangoon in 1955. I was seven then. My father is a captain now and he's working in the Social Relations Department of the government. We live in the center of the city, which is on the Rangoon River, in a building that has eight apartments in it. We are on the second floor and we have five rooms and two bathrooms. We have a servant and she has her own bedroom, kitchen, and bathroom. People in the villages often sleep on mats, but most city people sleep on beds as we do.

THE BRANCH CONVENT OF ST. JOHN'S

My home is about two miles away from school and it takes me about fifteen minutes to get there in a bus. We are not Catholics, but again my father sent me there, because it's such a good school. The school is a branch of the Convent of St. John's and it has 1,150 girls in it. I'm in the seventh grade now and I'm taking Burmese, English, moral instruction, geography, history, general science, and mathematics. I like my geography and English best, and I want to go on to the university and become a professor of geography and journalism.

Two of my sisters are in the same school. I've studied English for nine years now, but at home, of course, we speak Burmese. My father speaks English very well, but my mother doesn't.

A SCHOOL DAY

I get up every morning at five. First we have prayers together; then I do my homework for a half hour before I eat my breakfast, which consists of bread and coffee. School begins at seven thirty. We have a fifteen-minute recess at ten forty-five and I buy something to eat at the school canteen. Often I get a sandwich, or mohinga (like spaghetti), or fish. Classes end for the day at one in the afternoon, and then I go home for a big meal.

A plain Burmese meal is usually like this: boiled rice; *hingyo*, or soup; *ngapi*, which is a hot paste made of red chilies, garlic, onion, citron leaves, lemon, and other such things; the *to-sa-ya*, a salad of green vegetables; the *hin*, or curry of meat or fish. The Burmese people like fish and prawns (a kind of shrimp) the best. We have many sweets too, made of flour, nuts, raisins, and other fruits. With my big meal I may have bananas and papayas. I drink water.

In the afternoon I usually study for a half hour, help my mother with her work and take care of my youngest sister. I play basketball at school, but at home I usually play badminton for an hour. Then I study for another hour or two. At about six thirty we have another big meal. There's no television in Burma, but I usually listen to the radio, and almost always hear the Voice of America at eight thirty. I'm in bed at nine.

There's no school on Saturday and Sunday; but as we have no car I usually stay at home. I play outdoors, and go to the cinema, read the newspapers, and play snakes and ladders with my family. I'm very much interested in international affairs and in the United Nations. Most educated Burmans are interested in the United Nations, especially because a Burman is the Secretary General just now. I read regularly three American magazines: *Life, Time,* and *Newsweek.* I collect stamps and I draw and paint, portraits mostly. I might say also that one of my hobbies is travel, though up to date it has been an armchair kind of travel, since I've never been outside of Burma.

WE ARE MOSLEMS

Since my family is Moslem, I study the Mohammedan religion for a half hour every day. My father goes to the mosque, but women seldom go. There is a woman who comes to teach me. She lives near the mosque.

5. PAKISTAN

LAND OF THE TWO WINGS

THE DREAM OF PAKISTAN

Pakistan is the most populous Islamic state in the world. It has ninety-six million people, twice as many as Italy has, and almost as many as Japan has. This makes it the seventh largest nation in the world for population, and it is one of the most densely populated of all.

Yet twenty years ago Pakistan was only a rosy dream in the hearts of the Moslems of India. They remembered proudly the three centuries when Moslems ruled in India before the British came. But ever since then they had seen the Hindus surging ahead under the British *raj*, or reign. Hindus had come to occupy most of the high offices. They began to control the banks and business houses. They had had the best opportunities for a higher education. All this made the Moslems feel that they were receiving unfair treatment.

But the major reason for dissatisfaction was religion. The

great differences between Hinduism and Islam made it very difficult for the two groups to get along happily together. The Moslems believed in one God, the Hindus worshiped many. The Moslems believed that all men were brothers; the Hindus believed in castes with little in common among them. The Hindus thought that the cow was sacred; the Moslems ate the meat of the cow.

MOHAMMED ALI JINNAH

Pakistan was largely the work of one man, Mohammed Ali Jinnah. He turned the misty dream of Pakistan into a living reality. He said that "a hundred million Moslems were too many to be a minority." He demanded a homeland where Moslem ideals might find expression. The influential Congress Party of India was bitterly opposed to the whole plan, but the British government favored it. So on August 15, 1947, Britain withdrew from India and two separate dominions took its place.

Pakistan is no longer a dream.

Jinnah is called in Pakistan the "Father of the Nation." But he survived the realization of his dream by only one year. He died in September, 1948.

THE PROBLEMS OF PARTITION

The basis of partition was very simple in principle, but all kinds of difficulties arose from it. It had been agreed that all contiguous (that is, neighboring) Hindu areas should go to India and contiguous Moslem areas to Pakistan. This meant in reality two Pakistans instead of one. The region north of the Bay of Bengal became East Pakistan. It was almost completely surrounded on the land side by India. Only one other country bordered it, Burma, for about a hundred miles in the southeast.

A thousand miles to the west, on the other side of India, West Pakistan was created, bounded by the Arabian Sea in the south, by Iran and Afghanistan to the west, by a disputed territory of Jammu and Kashmir in the northeast, and by India in the southeast.

THE TWO WINGS

Two wings are fine to fly with if you're a bird, but there must be some connection between them. In the case of Pakistan there are a thousand miles of hostile territory between them, for India has never been happy about partition. By ship from West Pakistan's major port of Karachi to East Pakistan's major port of Chittagong, there is a three-thousand-mile voyage around the southern tip of India.

From the very beginning there was violence. Eight million Hindus and Sikhs left Pakistan for India, and ten million Moslems fled from India to Pakistan. There were many riots and terrible atrocities on both sides. Many of the skilled workers and experienced administrators, who were mainly Hindus, left Pakistan. There were few to take their places except the untrained men. Most of the factories in which raw products were processed, almost all the banks and business establishments, and the best educational institutions were in India, not in Pakistan.

Finally, there was for a time open warfare over Jammu and Kashmir. An uneasy truce has followed; but feelings are strong on both sides, and no solution of the problem is in sight.

Pakistan is a very new nation in a very old land. Its problems today are like those the United States would be facing if it had been split apart at the Mississippi River, and the Soviet

Union inserted in the gap. It's remarkable that Pakistan has survived at all.

TOO MUCH WATER

The two wings of Pakistan are very different from each other. East Pakistan has too much water. West Pakistan has too little. The great Brahmaputra flows from the northeast through India's province of Assam down into East Pakistan. From the northwest comes the Ganges, sacred to the Hindus, which flows into the Brahmaputra in East Pakistan. The united rivers pour their waters into the Bay of Bengal through a huge delta. Everywhere in East Pakistan there is water, too much of it. One of the great problems is to control it, and the United States is helping by financing the big Karnafuli Dam.

Because the land of the delta is low, there's always the danger of cyclones along the coast. In May, 1963, one of the worst of them all came with the monsoon season of rains. Twelve thousand people were drowned by wind-whipped waves that swept over their rice paddies and villages. The bamboo and thatch huts were blown away like matches in the violence of the storm.

TOO LITTLE WATER

West Pakistan also has great rivers, but it is largely a dry land with many deserts. The Indus is twenty-five hundred miles long. Cradled amidst the glaciers of Tibet, it flows down through the whole length of the land to the sea. It has a number of big branches, the most important of them being the five rivers of the *Punjab*, which actually means the five waters. These branches all have their origin outside West Pakistan, but the life of the people depends on them. Because of the division of Jammu and Kashmir between India and Pakistan, India has been able to tap some of these rivers for water that West Pakistan desperately needs.

So West Pakistan, with the help of the United States and other friends, is building many dams and barrages, canals, drainage ditches, and embankments to retain the surplus waters of the wet season so that they may flow over the parched lands in the dry season. It is also sinking many wells, and reclaiming lands that have become salty or exhausted. But all this takes hundreds of millions of dollars, and West Pakistan is still very poor.

CITIES

There are many thousands of little villages in Pakistan, but there are also some big cities. Karachi was a little fishing hamlet of mud huts a century ago. Now it has over 1.9 million people in it. It's a rapidly growing place, a boom city. People move into the new hotel rooms before the buildings are finished. This is symbolic, for the Pakistani are building a new country while they are living in it. Karachi was the capital of the whole country until August 1, 1960, when the capital was moved temporarily to Rawalpindi. A brand-new capital is now being constructed at Islamabad in the north. But Karachi will always be important. It is the country's great port with miles of piers. Fifteen international airlines land there.

Lahore, in the heart of West Pakistan, is the next largest city. It has about 1.3 million people and wonderful mausoleums, mosques, and gardens that date from the days of the Mogul emperors.

The capital and largest city of East Pakistan is Dacca. It has over 550,000 people.

THE GOVERNMENT

Pakistan is a federal republic, a member of the British Commonwealth. Its president is elected by a national assembly. In each wing of the divided country there is a provincial assembly.

It is an exciting adventure to watch a new country like Pakistan build its own future. All through the nation, in both wings of it, you see the dawn of a new day. The very contrasts you find everywhere tell their own story. There are turbaned tribesmen in the streets, pedicabs, and camel carts. But there are also motorcycles and the latest American cars. The old and the new sometimes blend in amusing ways, as when you see camels drawing a rubber-tired Mobilgas tank.

There are schools in little white-washed huts and classes meeting with their teachers in the open air on stony hillsides. But there are also fine new modern buildings, which would do honor to an American city. There are agricultural schools and universities, clinics and hospitals.

The future of Pakistan is bright with promise.

Our young people represent the two wings of the country. Najma Yusuf is an East Pakistan girl, who has spent part of her life in Chittagong, where the big steamers from all parts of the world come in, and part of it in Dacca. Taugeer Ahmad Quraishi is a boy living in Lahore. His father is a Moslem who was driven out of India after the partition.

The language of East Pakistan is Bengali, and in West Pakistan it is Urdu. But some phrases are the same in both languages. So both of these new friends of ours say to you, *Salam-o-Alaikum*, a greeting that means in both languages "Peace be with you."

A GIRL FROM EAST PAKISTAN
by Najma Yusuf

I WAS BORN IN INDIA

I am a Pakistani, but I was born in India at Gorakhpur in the province of Uttar Pradesh. That's up in the north of India in the Ganges River basin. Just across the border there in Nepal the Buddha was born at Lumbini. My father was employed in a sugar factory at Gorakhpur. I was born fourteen years ago.

I don't remember anything about India, however, for when I was three or four years old we moved to Chittagong in East Pakistan where I lived until I was eight or nine. My father was in the brick business there. He dealt in baked bricks, and the factory had its own brick fields. We have plenty of wood in East Pakistan so we can bake our bricks. In West Pakistan the people don't have much wood so their houses are usually made of unbaked mud bricks. The mud bricks are warmer in the winter and cooler in the summer, but when the rains come the walls wash away little by little.

CHITTAGONG

Chittagong is on the Bay of Bengal and it's the most important port in East Pakistan. There are wild elephants in the forests around Chittagong, and farther away in East Pakistan there are many Royal Bengal Tigers. Of course, the wild animals don't come near the cities.

Our house in Chittagong was not made of brick. It was made of bamboo, both the walls and the roof. Many houses there are made of bamboo, because the climate is warm. We had four rooms: two bedrooms, a dining room, and a living room. The toilet was outside, and there was a small, separate building for the kitchen. We had two trees in our yard and I had two cats to play with who liked to climb the trees. Their names were Pussy and Nog.

My mother was born in India and my father married her there. I have two brothers and four sisters. The oldest is a brother of twenty-five, who is married. He is now in the United States studying for his Ph.D. in California. He wants to be an electrical engineer. The youngest is a girl of twelve. I am the fifth oldest.

MY FIRST SCHOOL

I first went to school at Chittagong when I was five. This was a primary school and I was there for four years. It was a Catholic high school for girls, which included all the early grades. The school was about five miles from the center of the city, but my father had a car and drove me there. It took about fifteen minutes for the ride.

DACCA

From Chittagong I went to Dacca, the capital of East Pakistan. This was because my father had left the brick business and had become a field worker for the P.I.D.C. (Pakistan Industrial Development Corporation). He is now stationed in the north at Bogra and is working in the sugar division. We grow a lot of sugar in the north and east of my country, and my father travels all over that region. He goes by train. My father's new work isn't so nice for us, because he isn't home much now.

My country produces three million tons of sugar cane every year. Before partition the sugar factories were in what is now India. But the present policy of my government is to build factories in both East and West Pakistan.

MY CHILDHOOD GAMES

Except when I was very small I played only with girls. The games were hide-and-seek, handball, and skip-rope. At home I played caroms, snakes and ladders, and jackstones with other members of my family. I played with dolls too.

MY PRESENT SCHOOL

I go to a private school now run by Mrs. T. Johnston. It's for boys and girls, and there are about four hundred of us. All the teaching is in English.

Every day I get up at seven and after prayers (I'm a Moslem) I help to prepare the breakfast. We have *chapatis* (made of unleavened wheat flour, flat like pancakes), eggs, and tea. Then I study at home until ten. From ten to eleven thirty I listen to the radio at home. We have lunch at eleven thirty. This is usually a rice curry with meat or fish, tomatoes, and cucumbers. I have water to drink. Then I catch a rickshaw for my school. The rickshaw is a little two-wheeled carriage with room for two on the seat, pulled by a man in front riding on a bicycle. It takes about twenty minutes to get to school in this way. School is from twelve thirty to four thirty. After that I go home. I play a little outside the house, study from six to nine, and then have my dinner, which is just like my lunch. I'm in bed at ten fifteen.

I'm in sixth standard now, taking Urdu, the principal language of West Pakistan, English, arithmetic, algebra, geometry, history, geography, and general science. I like English best of all, but I haven't decided yet what I want to do after finishing school.

Primary schooling is free in Pakistan now and compulsory, but no one would have to make me go. I like my school very much.

UNIFORMS AND DRESSES

The boys in school wear navy-blue pants, which may be short or long, and a white shirt. We girls wear a uniform made up of a *shalwar*, a *kameez*, and *dupata*. The shalwar is a pair of white cotton trousers, which go down to the shoes. The kameez is a blue overdress, which falls to the knees. It has elbow-length sleeves. The dupata is a strip of white cloth about two inches wide that comes over one shoulder, passes under the middle of the belt in front, then up over the other shoulder. In back both ends come down under the belt and hang loose there. We wear our hair in long braids.

At home I wear just the shalwar and kameez, and my dresses are usually colored.

OTHER ACTIVITIES

East Pakistan has many rivers which are full of fish. I don't fish myself, but I do go boating on a river near the city. Sometimes I visit other members of my family, or my girl friends. I don't dance or play music.

Our long vacation is in September and October. Sometimes during this long vacation I go back to Chittagong, where I still have an uncle living.

As most of the people in Pakistan are Moslems and my country thinks of itself as an Islamic state, I am taught my religion in school. We celebrate the month of fasting which is called in Arabic states *Ramadan*. We call it *Ramzan* here. During this month we never eat between sunrise and sunset, though we are allowed to have cold drinks. We have a big meal in the evening, and if we wish we can have another in the morning before daybreak.

Ramzan is followed by *Id*, which is a very happy time. Then we get new clothes to wear, make many calls, and have very good things to eat. Two months later comes another Moslem festival called *Baqreed*. Then the family has someone from the Mosque come to kill a goat. The meat is divided into three parts. One is for the family, one is for our friends, and one is for the poor. Actually more than a third of the meat goes to the poor.

MY LANGUAGES

I speak Urdu and English. I can understand Bengali also, but I don't speak it very well. Some of the phrases in Urdu and Bengali are just the same. We both say *Salam-o-Alaikum*, which means "Peace be with you." This is a greeting for any time of the day. *Khoda Hafiz* means "God be with you," in both languages. That's how we say good-by.

I LIVE IN WEST PAKISTAN
by Taugeer Ahmad Quraishi

MY PARENTS ARE REFUGEES

When India was divided and a new Moslem state of Pakistan was set up in 1947, there was a great deal of trouble, terrible confusion, and much suffering.

My father, whose name is Muzaffar Quraishi, was born in Amritsar, which is now in the Indian part of the Punjab. He studied psychology in Amritsar. When partition came my father did not leave Amritsar with other Moslem refugees. The Indian government seized the house he owned and all his belongings and drove him out. He did not lose the money he had in the bank, but he lost everything else. So he came to Lahore, which is not far west of Amritsar, but in the Pakistani part of the Punjab. The Pakistan government gave him an apartment, but he had to pay rent for it. He is now a professor of psychology in Government College in Lahore.

My mother was also born in Amritsar. She married my father before he was driven out. I have two older sisters and two younger brothers. My oldest sister, who is twenty, is in college but not in my father's college. The rest of us are all in lower schools. My youngest brother is nine.

Our apartment is on the second floor of a brick house in the very crowded center of the city, a few steps from one of the busiest main streets. I was born here in this house thirteen years ago, and I've lived here ever since. I don't remember anything about my very early life. Of course, I played the games all boys play: cricket, hockey, and football. I have always liked cricket best of all, but I've never been on a regular team. There is a playground about five minutes' walk from my house, and when the boys go there to play they make up their own teams and have a game.

My full name is Tauqeer Ahmad Quraishi. My nickname is Cuckoo.

THE CATHEDRAL HIGH SCHOOL

I have been attending this school ever since I was three years old. I began in the nursery school, and now, ten years later, I am in the junior seventh standard. I'm ahead of most of the boys of my age, for I've had two double promotions. I skipped the upper kindergarten and the second standard. The last class in the school is the senior Cambridge.

My father sent me to this school because it's such a good one. It's just eighty years old now and has over twelve hundred boys and girls. The headmaster is English, but most of the teachers are Pakistanis. We have both men and women teachers. The school has a simple Christian service, but we don't have to go. Moslem teaching is given twice a week.

At school I wear a uniform: gray shorts, light blue shirt, white socks, and black shoes. On special days we wear green coats. Our school badge has the motto of the school on it, *Facta non verba,* "Deeds and not words."

AN ORDINARY SCHOOL DAY

I get up at six thirty and then I have my breakfast of bread, eggs, and milk. School begins at seven fifteen in the summer, and eight in the winter. It takes about ten minutes to walk to school, but I make it in three minutes on my bicycle. We have a half-hour break at ten thirty and I usually get some coffee or tea. School closes at one fifteen for the day. So I'm home for lunch, which usually consists of rice curry with chicken, beef, mutton, or fish. Sometimes I have a green salad. For dessert I have pudding or ice cream. I drink milk.

In the afternoon I go out to play for an hour or two, and I usually study for a couple of hours. I listen to the radio, too. We have dinner at eight in the evening, and this is like our midday meal. We get good fish from the Ravi River. After dinner I study a little and then I go to bed at nine thirty or ten.

We have school on Saturday. On Sunday I play most of the day, but after six in the evening I do some more homework.

WE ARE MOSLEMS

My father teaches the psychology of religion, and he doesn't go to the mosque. Boys like myself seldom go until they're sixteen or seventeen.

There are some famous mosques in Lahore, and I have visited them all. The Badshahi Mosque in the Red Fort is said to be the largest in the world. This mosque, which has tall minarets and white domes, was built by Aurangzeb, the last of the great Mogul emperors. He lies buried in a magnificent mausoleum in the middle of a very large garden.

The best known of the Lahore gardens are the Shalimar Gardens, which were laid out by the first of the great Mogul emperors, Shah Jahan. There are three terraces and five hundred fountains. This emperor loved fountains because they cooled the air in the hot weather.

Shah Jahan had a son, Prince Selim, who fell in love with a slave girl named Anarkali. His father caught them smiling at each other, and he was so angry that a slave girl would even lift her eyes to the emperor's son that he sentenced her to death on the spot. He had her walled up and buried alive right there. Selim later became the Emperor Jehangir; but he never ceased to love the beautiful slave girl. So, as Emperor, he built a mosque over Anarkali's tomb.

The Moslem festival I like best is *Eid*, the happy time that follows our month of fasting, Ramadan. We all go visiting during Eid, and everywhere we go we get a cold drink and Pakistani sweets. These are something between cake and candy.

MURREE HILL STATION

Our long vacation comes in June and July. Then the family always goes to a summer resort in the hills, called Murree Hill Station. We take rooms in a hotel for the season. The place is seventy-five hundred feet high and the mountains around it go up to eight and nine thousand feet. I like to climb in these mountains. I'm very fond of horseback riding too, and I often hire a horse. I like photography, and I know the birds, the flowers, the trees, and the animals. Finally, I like to paint landscapes in water colors.

LANGUAGES AND TRAVEL

Punjabi is my mother tongue, but I speak Urdu and English also.

I've never traveled much, just to Karachi on the Arabian Sea when I was small.

6. NEPAL

LAND OF THE
TALL, YOUNG MOUNTAINS

LONG AGO AND FAR AWAY

Sandwiched in between the big giants of India and China is the little independent kingdom of Nepal. The country is a fairly regular rectangle about 500 miles long and 150 miles wide. Its 54,000 square miles make it just about the size of Illinois or Iowa. It has some nine million people.

Nepal has always been a very difficult country to reach. Approaching it from the south you have to cross hot, steaming jungles full of dangerous animals. From the north you have to cross the Himalayas, the highest mountains on the globe. This long range on Nepal's northern frontier has twenty-five peaks over 22,000 feet high, with Mount Everest, the loftiest in the world, rising to 29,028 feet. This is the ridge-pole of our planet.

Most of those who would have made that long, difficult journey into Nepal, at least from the south, were prevented from doing so. Until the end of the Second World War, the country was a forbidden kingdom. Only a handful of foreigners were allowed to come in by special invitation of the prime minister. The door to Nepal was usually shut and locked to the outside world.

So the country was little modernized. It was a primitive land. When you arrived you found you had gone backward to a distant past. Nepal was a land of long ago as well as a land of far away.

THE TERAI

There are three distinct regions in Nepal. In the south on the border of India is the Terai, a strip of flat, malarial land about 350 feet above the sea. A large bit of it consists of dense jungles and forests, where tigers, cobras, leopards, elephants, and rhinoceroses roam. This was an exciting hunting ground for the kings and nobles of Nepal and their invited guests. Tiger hunts were particularly popular. Elephants tramped through the bush, the men on their backs beating drums and sticks. These beaters drove the tiger into a clearing, where other elephants waited with hunters perched on *howdahs* (platforms on the elephants' backs). When the tiger found himself surrounded by the big, ponderous beasts, he usually charged one of them with his fangs bared. Just as he leaped, the rifles fired. And that was the end for that day of a very dangerous sport.

The Terai, however, is not all jungle and forest. About two-thirds of the crop land of Nepal is here and one-third of all the people. Nine-tenths of the population are farmers. They grow rice, sugar cane, wheat, vegetables, fruits, cotton, and tobacco.

THE LOWER HIMALAYAS

The Terai is the first step up from the plains of northern India. The next step is the Lower Himalayan Region. There are many virgin forests here and much valuable timber. There is much grazing land for goats and other livestock. The mountains run up to about eleven thousand feet.

In the midst of the second region is the Khatmandu Valley. This is the very heart of Nepal. More than 450,000 people live in the valley, and about 110,000 in the city. Most of the Nepalese use the word *Nepal* just for the valley, not for the country as a whole.

THE HIGH HIMALAYAS

The Lower Himalayas lead to the third and final step, the High Himalayas. Five of the highest mountains in the world are here, all of them over 26,400 feet. The small villages are, of course, in the valleys, but even there the weather gets bitterly cold in the winter. On the stony land around the villages the people grow wheat, barley, and potatoes. They keep sheep, goats, and yaks. There are seldom any roads at all, just rough trails running up and down from village to village.

MOUNT EVEREST

The Tibetans call the mountain *Chomolungma*, the "Mother of the World." They say the gods live there. But I think you'd agree that any place where the temperature drops to 50 degrees below zero fahrenheit, and gales rage up to 150 miles an hour is a rather bleak dwelling place for the gods.

The early attempts to climb the mountain were from the northern, or Tibetan, side. All of them failed.

In 1953, however, the New Zealander, Edmund Hillary, and a guide from the Sherpa tribe, named Tenzing Norkay, finally conquered the peak and stood on the top of the world. In 1956 a successful Swiss expedition followed. Then a Soviet-Chinese climbing party claimed that in 1960 they had placed a statue of Mao Tse-tung, the Chinese Communist leader, on the top of the mountain. Most people doubted it.

Late in February, 1963, a great party, with 895 Nepalese as porters and 32 Sherpas for work on the heights, started out from Khatmandu to challenge once again this formidable mountain foe. The expedition was organized by the National Geographic Society, the National Science Foundation, and various departments of the United States government. The trek to the base of the mountain was 180 miles long. Finally the climb began and at eight o'clock on the morning of May 1, 1963, James Warren Whittaker, an American, and Nwang Gombu, a Sherpa, stood on the icy summit. Whittaker was a great, strapping fellow, six feet, five inches tall and 210 pounds in weight. Nwang Gombu was the nephew of Tenzing Norkay, who ten years earlier had accompanied Hillary to the top. They looked around carefully, but they could see no sign of the Mao Tse-tung statue. When Whittaker came down to the base again he had lost thirty pounds.

On May 23 four more Americans from the same expedition reached the summit. Barry Bishop and Luther Jerstad came up by the South Col, the route followed by the earlier successful climbers. Thomas Hornbein and William Unsoeld climbed up by the West Ridge, which was so dangerous that no one had ever tried to climb it before. The four men met at nine in the evening just below the summit. It was too late to descend, so they spent the night huddled together in the open.

Time Magazine says that there was an American traffic jam on the top of the world that day.

THE LAND OF THE MIGHTY RIVERS

Down from these white towers, Everest, Annapurna, Dhauragiri, and their gigantic comrades of the skies, swirl mighty rivers, bearing in their turbulent waters millions of tons of silt to the Terai and the River Ganges. The greatest of these streams is the Kosi. Perhaps you have never heard of this river, yet it drains almost twenty-four thousand square miles. The much better known Ganges of Northern India drains only nine thousand square miles.

MANY TRIBES

Around the capital at Khatmandu most of the people belong to the Newar tribe. These are possibly descendants of the earliest settlers in Nepal. They are very clever craftsmen. They carve beautiful statues and build lovely temples.

In the outlying valleys most of the people of the kingdom think of themselves not as Nepalese, but as members of tribes. They are Gurungs, Tamangs, Bhutias. The Gurkhas are famous. They came originally from India and conquered Khatmandu in 1769. Then for many years they ruled the whole country. They were strong and brave soldiers. In both world wars they fought on the side of the Allies. There are Gurkha regiments in the British army. They have fought in Africa recently under the banner of the United Nations.

The Sherpas have also become very well known. They live in the mountain valleys and are used to high altitudes. That is why they have been employed so often by the mountaineers.

THE LIFE OF THE PEOPLE

Most of the people are farmers. They are often very primitive, using ancient tools. So they are among the poorest people in the world. There is a great deal of illness and very few doctors. Most of the people do not live beyond their thirty-fifth birthday. Only one in ten can read or write. There is very little industry, very few factories.

The land is cultivated up the slopes of the mountains as high as twelve thousand feet.

In the harsh winters thousands of the men and boys leave Nepal and go south to work in India. They take with them some of their products, sell them over the border in India, buy railway tickets to Indian ports, work as stevedores for a few months, and then go home again. On the way they spend the money they have earned for Indian goods, which they take back to their villages.

CLOTHES

The hill women wear very full long skirts, which are usually red. Their tight jackets are also usually of bright colors. They wear many strings of coins and beads, brass or coin earrings, silver and glass bracelets. They let their hair hang down over each shoulder in two braids and throw a scarf over their heads.

A well-dressed gentleman in Khatmandu will wear light, tight-fitting cotton trousers that look like riding breeches, a long shirt that ties over the left shoulder and on the left side at the waist line, with a belt around it. This shirt may reach almost to his knees and hangs down over his trousers. On his head he wears a cap that looks a bit like a stocking, though it's only about four or five inches high on one side and a little lower on the other. It's a rather nice-looking costume. But then, if he is a well-to-do gentleman, he wears a European coat over that. This makes him look rather funny to a westerner, just as if the westerner were wearing a suit with the tails of his shirt hanging out below the coat in front and back.

A LIVING GODDESS

The people of Nepal are about 70 per cent Hindus and 30 per cent Buddhists. The country is full of temples, especially Hindu temples. You find them everywhere, sometimes thickly clustered together. There's a square in Khatmandu that must have a dozen or more big ones, with many others in the same neighborhood. Some of these are very important from the point of view of archaeology, yet almost all of them are in a state of great neglect. Unless something is done to preserve them many of them will come tumbling down before too long.

There is a living goddess in Khatmandu, called Kumari. She is a young girl who has never seen blood. Through her the goddess whose name she bears may speak. She is usually kept out of the sight of people. But once a year she is paraded through the streets and even the king worships her. The moment she has seen blood another girl is chosen to take her place.

Gautama Buddha, the founder of Buddhism, was born in Nepal.

UNTOUCHABLES

Hinduism has a very rigid caste system. The highest caste is that of the Brahmins. The lowest is that of the Untouchables, and the Brahmins will have nothing to do with them. If you had gone to Nepal a year or two ago you would have been surprised to find that you were considered an Untouchable by many people. All foreigners were.

As a distinguished foreigner you might have been invited to visit a Brahmin family. Perhaps you would have seen the family eating together, while you received nothing at all in the way of food. Then if your host were very polite he might have asked if you would like to have something to eat before the women of the family ate.

In 1963, however, a new legal code was adopted that abolished the caste of Untouchables, and permitted marriage across the caste lines. All citizens, the code said, were regarded as equals before the law.

THE KING AND THE RANAS

The people of Nepal are wretchedly poor, but the city of Khatmandu is full of huge and stately palaces. So we come to the story of the *Ranas*. This was the family that ruled Nepal for about a hundred years. They held the king a kind of prisoner. They kept the foreigners out of the country, because they feared outsiders might spread discontent and stir up trouble among the people.

There were three classes of Ranas, *A*, *B*, and *C*. *A* consisted of the prime minister and his immediate family. *B* was the other branches of the family. *C* was the children of the un-married mothers in the harem.

All these Ranas built palaces, and there were about two thousand of them. Class *A* had to have at least a hundred rooms. Class *B* had to have about seventy. Class *C* was content with forty.

Above the Ranas was the king, but he was just a figurehead without power. Finally he escaped to India, and in 1950 India led the king back and overthrew the Ranas. But they still have enormous wealth and great power.

ROPEWAYS

In the old days there was a narrow-gauge railway that led from the border of India into the country for twenty-nine miles. There you took a bus for another twenty-eight miles. Finally you hired a horse, or a pony, or a litter to carry you another sixteen miles over two passes, each seven thousand feet high, to reach the capital.

Then a ropeway was built. This was a strong cable strung on towers, on which little platforms traveled. On these plat-forms tons of supplies in sacks and boxes could be carried. The ropeway was operated by electricity.

Everything else had to be carried on the backs of men and women. It was a strange sight to see a motor car carried on a pole platform by sixty to a hundred porters.

THE UNITED STATES HELPS

The United States has now built a second ropeway, which can carry twenty-five tons of food an hour on platforms over the mountains to Khatmandu.

This is only one of many ways in which the United States

is trying to strengthen and modernize Nepal. We are helping to build dams, and roads, and bridges; to clear the jungle, to fight malaria, to provide better breeds of sheep and poultry.

Other countries are also helping.

It is now possible to fly from Calcutta in India and from Dacca in East Pakistan to Khatmandu.

Our young people represent the two great religions of Nepal. Indira Devi Chalise is the daughter of a Hindu priest living in an old valley village. Man Bahadur Lama belongs to the Tamang tribe, which came from the high mountains in the north. He is a Buddhist and lives close to the most famous Buddhist temple in Nepal.

MY FATHER IS A HINDU PRIEST
by Indira Devi Chalise

I WORSHIP MY BROTHERS

The most important festival in the whole year for us Hindus of Nepal is the festival of Tihar. It comes at the end of our year and lasts for five days. On each day we have something different to worship. The first day we worship the crow, though nobody seems to know exactly why. It's just an ancient custom. We are supposed to pray in the temple for the crow, to think of it in a kindly way, and to feed it.

The second day we worship dogs. People put garlands round their necks and feed them.

The third day it's the cow we worship. Of course, it's not difficult to understand why.

The fourth day may seem very strange to you, for then we worship ourselves. We remember that we are part of the universe, that God is everywhere, and so is in us.

Finally on the fifth day we worship our brothers. We draw circular patterns on the floor in front of our brothers with colored chalk and decorate them with flowers which we have brought in on brass trays. Then we hang ropes of flowers around the necks of our brothers, pour oil on their hair and kneel down before them. After the worship has ended we have a feast, perhaps of rice, beans, curds, and hard-boiled eggs. Finally, everyone gets some betel nuts, lime, and spices, wrapped up in green leaves to eat. All the men eat first, and then the women are allowed to eat.

THE FESTIVAL OF DASAI

This is another festival that comes in October or November. It celebrates the work of all the goddesses. We sacrifice a goat then and worship in the temple. There are feasts and dances too. The young people go from door to door, singing and dancing in honor of Durga Bhavani, the goddess of victory.

I LIVE IN AN HISTORIC VILLAGE

The village of Besi Gaon Gokerna, not far from Khatmandu, has buildings in it that go back to the sixth century of the Christian Era. It has also a very beautiful Hindu temple, high above the Bagamati River, which flows by Khatmandu. The god Shiva always rode on a bull, and in front of the temple is a statue of a bull.

My father is a priest in the village and attached to this temple. The priests hold their office for life. There is no school for priests. The traditions, the knowledge of the sacred writings, the directions for the ceremonies of worship, are passed on from the priests to those who want to become priests. My father conducts services in the temple, visits the sick, is present at marriages and funerals, and helps to cremate the dead down by the river.

My father is married and has ten children. I have seven

sisters and two brothers. I'm the sixth among the girls, and I have one older brother and one younger brother. My father was born in this village and so was I. My mother was born in another village some distance away. I know the exact date of my birth in my calendar, but I don't know how to change that into the European calendar. I'm about twelve years of age.

OUR HOUSE IS OF MUD BRICKS

Our house is in the center of the village. It has two floors and a tile roof. On the ground floor there is just the kitchen and a cow shed. We have two cows, one buffalo, and six sheep. We keep the cows and the buffalo just for the milk. We don't sell any of the milk and we don't kill any of the cattle. We sell the wool from the sheep, and we kill the male sheep sometimes for the meat. From the milk we make butter and cheese.

We cook our food over a fire which burns on the floor of the kitchen, and I have to gather wood for the fire. We have kerosene lamps. There's no running water in the house. I bring water from the village, and on ordinary days I take a bath in the house. But on special days I go down to the river to bathe. We have a small walled garden.

I wear a *suruwal* and a *kurtha*. The first is a long pair of cotton trousers. The second is the long shirt with short sleeves that falls to my knees. On my forehead I have a little red circle. This shows that I've been to the temple. When I was a baby two months old my ears were pierced and now I wear earrings in them. A little later a small hole was made on the left side of my nose and I wear a gold ornament there. This is called a *nak-fuli*.

MY FATHER WAS MY FIRST TEACHER

When I was six my father began to teach me at home. He taught me to read, to write, and to do arithmetic. I did not begin to go to the village school until I was eleven. I have been there for two years now. I'm studying Nepali, arithmetic, geography, and science. After another year I'll have to go to a different school. I like my language studies best, and I'd like to go into the service of the government.

Every morning I'm up at six. I read for a little while, then I worship the gods and goddesses that are in my home, and finally I have my breakfast. School lasts from ten to four, and then I go home to have a little snack. After that I help my mother and we have our dinner at seven. I go to bed at eight.

WEEKENDS

Friday is a half holiday, and Saturday is a full holiday. When I was small I used to play with dolls in the house, and I played outdoors with the other girls. Now I'm too old to play any more. So when I'm free I help my mother in the house. With our family of twelve she has a lot to do. I often go shopping for her. On Sunday we are in school again.

Most of the time I worship at home, but sometimes I go to the temple too.

A BUDDHIST BOY IN NEPAL
by Man Bahadur Lama

THE ALL-SEEING EYES

The great temple of Buddha at Bodhinath is really a part of my life. It's the largest Buddhist temple in Nepal and nobody knows how old it is. It goes back before the story of Nepal was written down. Some people think that a Tibetan lama who came from Lhasa died there and that the temple was built on the spot where he was either buried or cremated. Other people say that the temple contains some part of Buddha's body, some of his ashes or hairs from his head, but nobody seems to know what. During the winter months great pilgrimages come here from long distances, for this is the most famous Buddhist temple in the whole country.

It used to be kept in repair by the Buddhist lamas in Tibet, but that stopped when the Chinese took over Tibet and drove the Dalai Lama out of the country. Now the pilgrims themselves clean away the weeds and mosses that grow during the rainy season, repair the cracks in the concrete, and repaint the divine eyes.

The great temple is round and in the middle of a circular plaza. There are three broad platforms or terraces that rise one above the other. Then on the topmost one there rests a huge, concrete hemisphere, which is ninety feet across. From the middle of this there rises a square tower, which is called a *toran*, and on each of the four sides there are two huge eyes, painted in blue and white enamel, that watch the village, the fields, the people, my house, and me all the time. Above the toran is a *stupa*, which comes to a point 135 feet above the ground.

All around the base of the temple there are prayer wheels which contain hundreds of prayers from the Buddhist holy writings. As people walk around the temple they turn the prayer wheels, and that makes the prayers go up to heaven. People also have small prayer wheels that they hold in their hands and twirl as they walk about. In this way they can pray as they are going about their business. There is a road that goes all around the temple, and on the other side of the road are places where the monks pray and conduct services.

MY FATHER IS A FARMER

Our house is made of mud bricks. It has two floors and a thatched roof. We occupy the whole house. There are four rooms and the house has three windows in back and two in front. At night we use kerosene lamps. We have two kitchens: one is for the ordinary cooking, and one is used to make beer, which we call *chhang*. There is an outside toilet.

Six of us live there, my father and mother, two older brothers, one of whom is married, and myself. I have no sister.

My father is a farmer. He has about an acre of land, which is far away from the house. He grows rice and maize. Last year he grew wheat, but he doesn't do that often, for the wheat is bad for the rice. He doesn't grow vegetables on his land. We buy them in the village market. My father is only a tenant farmer, and he has to give half of everything he grows to the landlord. So things are hard for us and we are very poor.

THE TAMANG TRIBE

We belong to the Tamang tribe, which is often called the "Lamas." My father was born in this village, and my mother in a village not far away. As a matter of fact, the whole village of Bodhinath is made up of my people. But originally we came from the mountains in the north, and we are very much like the Sherpas, who also live in those high mountains and have become famous as porters for the mountain climbers. We are all of Tibetan origin, as you can tell by looking at my face.

THIS IS MYSELF

My name is Man Bahadur Lama. I was born in this village of Bodhinath fourteen years ago, but I don't know the exact date. When I was small I used to help my mother, bring water from the spring, and do a little cooking. Sometimes I helped my father on the farm too. My father has three oxen, but he has no cows. He's busy all the year through. He plants his maize in May and his rice in July.

THE VILLAGE SCHOOL

I've been in school for four or five years now. I speak Tamang at home, for that's my mother tongue; but at school I'm learning to speak Nepali, the national language. The rest of the time we have what we call general knowledge. That means I'm learning a little history, a little geography, a little arithmetic, and very soon I shall start to learn a little English.

I get up at six and have my bath outside the house. Then I have some tea, after which I do some homework. I help my mother cook the breakfast, which is always rice and curry, though sometimes we have meat or fish with it. I have some green salad also, but no fruit.

School is from ten to four. At one o'clock I go home for a snack and at four I'm through school for the day. After that I go shopping and play with my friends. Then I help my mother get the evening meal, which is the other big meal of the day. In the evening during the festivals I always go back to the temple to see the priests dance.

Saturday is a school holiday. In the morning and the evening I go to the temple. I burn joss sticks, bring offerings, turn the prayer wheels, and worship.

We have school on Sunday.

After one more year in the primary school I shall go to the high school. I'd like to learn more from books and maybe I'll be a teacher someday. I'd like very much to do that.

7. INDIA

THE GREAT ASIAN SUB-CONTINENT

INDIA'S GEORGE WASHINGTON

His real name was Mohandas Karamchand Gandhi, but very few in India called him that. To millions he was a holy man, a saint. Many people called him Mahatma, or great soul, but Gandhi did not like that title. Still others called him affectionately Gandhiji. Gandhi liked that diminutive. Gandhi is dead now, but his picture is everywhere in his country.

He was born in 1869 and became a lawyer. But he soon gave up his practice to champion the cause of his people, first in South Africa, later in India. He gave up all western ways, lived very simply, and dressed in a loin cloth and shawl. The latter half of his life was spent fighting the evil customs of his time, like untouchability, and striving for India's freedom. He believed in the brotherhood of all men and the fatherhood of one God. When he preached he used the Koran, the Christian Bible, and the Hindu scriptures.

He came to believe firmly in the principle of nonviolence. His influence was so great that just by threatening to fast to his death he was able to secure many reforms.

The freedom for which he worked so hard was finally granted by Great Britain. But Gandhi believed that Moslems and Hindus should and could live happily together, and he was greatly disappointed by the partition of the great country he loved into separate Hindu and Moslem states.

He used to hold an evening prayer meeting wherever he happened to be. He was conducting one not far from New Delhi in 1948, when he was shot by a Hindu who blamed him for partition, though Gandhi did not want partition. The place where he was cremated, according to Hindu custom, is now marked by a concrete stone and surrounded by an iron fence. Here at dawn and at sunset people come to bring flowers and to offer prayer.

Gandhi still has enormous influence in India. He gave to his country a sense of purpose, a feeling of unity.

THE DIAMOND

What is this land for which Gandhi lived and died? It's shaped like an elongated diamond. This is perhaps symbolic, since India used to be the world's largest producer of diamonds. Its southern tip is Cape Comorin. Its northern tip, about two thousand miles away, is the high Himalayas. The width of India is about eighteen hundred miles. The country occupies about 1,220,000 square miles. India is, you see, a huge country, just about one-third the size of the United States.

On the southeast it is bounded by Burma, East Pakistan, and the Bay of Bengal, on the southwest by the Arabian Sea, on the northwest by Pakistan and the disputed region of

Jammu and Kashmir, and on the northeast by Tibet, Nepal, Sikkim, and Bhutan.

India's population is also huge, exceeded only by that of China. About 440 million people live in it, and the population is increasing by about 2 per cent a year, or about nine million people. While the country is about one-third the size of the United States, it has about three times as many mouths to feed.

PLAINS AND PLATEAUS

Up in the north is the Hindustan Plain which stretches across the big peninsula. From ninety to three hundred miles wide, this is the most fertile part of the nation. About half the people of India live on this plain, growing rice, sugar cane, wheat, and cotton. India is the sixth largest wheat-producing country in the world, and the fifth largest sugar-producing country. It has more cattle than any other land, 257 million of them. But this does not add to the wealth of the people. Most of the cattle are scrawny, ill-fed beasts, giving only about a quart of milk a day. They may not be killed, for cows are sacred to the Hindus. So both people and cattle go hungry. The land could only support 60 per cent of the cattle it has. You see them everywhere, lying on the sidewalks and in the middle of the streets. Traffic must find a way around them. They must not be disturbed.

About 82 per cent of the people of India are farmers.

MOUNTAINS AND RIVERS

Up in the far north are the mighty Himalayas, rising like a company of great saints, their heads encircled by shining halos of snow.

South of the Hindustan Plain more mountains rise, stretching across the peninsula and leveling off somewhat to form the Daccan Plateau. Mountains in the southeast and southwest, just back of the coast, come together at the southern tip of the land. The plateau is a triangle surrounded by mountains. Here on this higher land the farmers grow peanuts, millet, and other grains.

In the southwest the mountains fall to the sea in great steps called the Western Ghats. Here is the place where coconuts and teakwood flourish. This is the Malabar Coast. Pepper and other spices go from here all over the world.

On the opposite, or southeast, side of the sub-continent are the Eastern Ghats. This is the Coromandel Coast with the important city of Madras.

There are many rivers in all parts of the country. The most important are the Brahmaputra, which flows from east to west through Tibet before turning south into Assam and East Pakistan, and the Ganges, which the Indians call the "Ganga," flowing from northwest to southeast before it enters East Pakistan to join the Brahmaputra. Many other streams flow into these rivers. In the far north are the important Punjab rivers that flow through Jammu and Kashmir into West Pakistan.

THE CLIMATE

India is everywhere a land of climatic contrasts. Assam in the east is one of the wettest spots on earth with a rainfall of four hundred inches a year. In the west is the Thar, or Indian, desert, which is exceedingly dry. The south is a place of extreme tropical heat, and the north is a place of arctic cold. About half of India is in the tropical zone, and the other half in the temperate. But even the temperate zone is often exceedingly hot.

THE MONSOONS

The monsoons are the seasonal winds that blow from the southwest in the spring, usually bringing heavy rains; in the fall they come from the northeast and bring winds but very little rain. The people wait impatiently for the southwest monsoon, because if the monsoon rains fail, as they sometimes do, the people die of starvation. Famines are common in India. In the great Bengal famine in 1943 more than a million people died in Calcutta alone. You can imagine, therefore, the delight of everyone when dark clouds first appear on the horizon, lightning begins to dart here and there, big drops come splashing down, and the dusty fields turn dark and wet. The children rush out to get soaked in the cooling downpour, the men and women stand in the doorways to laugh and shout. In the evening the people gather outdoors or in the community houses of the villages to dance and sing and rejoice.

Unfortunately the rains come often in torrents and run off quickly. Frequently there are disastrous floods that do much damage. One of India's major problems is to train the rivers, to dam up the waste waters, and to spread them over the land in irrigation ditches.

During the last ten years India has built many dams on the rivers, enough to irrigate over thirty million acres, and to produce a lot of hydroelectric power. Happily India is strong in manpower, too strong, indeed, for there is much unemployment.

THE PEOPLE OF INDIA

The people have dark skins, especially in the south, but they are not Negroid. They belong to the white, or Caucasian, stock. There are two great language groups. In the south is the Dravidian group. These languages were spoken all over the subcontinent in the early days. Then, some three thousand years ago, the Aryans came in from the north and conquered the people. They were a warlike race with light complexions. Many of the native peoples were pushed to the south. Those that remained in the north mingled with the Aryans, and the result was the lighter skins we find there.

The languages in the north belong to the Aryan family. Most European and many Indian languages come from the Sanskrit, the language of the earliest sacred literature. Hindi belongs to this group. It's the most important language in northern India, spoken by more than a hundred million people. The government hopes that soon Hindi will be spoken by everybody. But that time is probably far away, for there are now fourteen major languages in India and hundreds of minor ones. The government estimates that there are 845 of these less important tongues.

THE CASTES

Castes are forbidden by the new Indian constitution, but they still exist. Below the four major castes are other humbler groups down to the Untouchables. These are the laundrymen, the scavengers, and other people engaged in the dirtiest and most disagreeable work. One of these groups is so low that its members are not supposed to show their faces by daylight. Gandhi tried to dignify the Untouchables. He called them the *harijan*, the children of God.

THE D.I.P. BELT

Whether they are Untouchables or not, the lot of most Indians is desperately bad. India made many of the native

princes and foreign administrators fabulously rich, but it hasn't
done much for the great mass of the people. They live in what
is called the D.I.P. belt. That means the belt of disease, igno-
rance, and poverty. Their life expectancy is about forty. About
three-quarters of the babies are said to die in their first year.
Seventy-five per cent of the people cannot read or write. The
average income is sixty-nine dollars a year. The first problem
of India is the amazing growth of its population. Thousands
of people sometimes live on a single square mile of land. Yet
the present Prime Minister of India used to say that his country was underpopulated. The reverse is certainly true today.

THE INDUS VALLEY CIVILIZATION

We once thought that western civilization had its origins
only in Egypt, in the valley of the Tigris and Euphrates, and in
the river valleys of China. But in the nineteen-twenties another civilization, which grew up quite separately, was discovered in the Indus Valley. It was certainly forty-five hundred years old, and probably much older. The ruins of an
extensive culture were discovered at Mohenjo-Daro on the
banks of the lower Indus and farther north at Harappa. These
were large cities, inhabited by people who were in no way
primitive. Buildings were made of burnt bricks. The streets
had excellent drainage. There were public granaries, assembly
halls, and baths. Indeed every well-to-do family had a private
bath at home.

They had their own writing too, a pictorial writing that has
never been deciphered. They did lovely carving and made
beautiful pottery. Their seals were famous. They had golden
jewelry, musical instruments, and toys for the children.

This civilization came to a sudden and terrible end. Some
invaders from the north, probably the Aryans, swept down

upon it, slaughtered men, women, and children, and destroyed the ancient cities.

After that came silent centuries. They have left no trace, no records behind them.

INVADERS AND FOREIGN RULERS

In the latter part of the fourth century B.C. Alexander the Great, who has been called a "Whirlwind in Human Form," arrived in the Indus Valley, after fighting his way through the Middle East in one of history's greatest marches. He overran the Punjab, but at the Ravi River his men revolted. They would go no farther. So Alexander had to turn back. He died of a fever in 323 B.C.; he was only thirty-three years of age.

The next great conqueror was Asoka, who ruled in nearly all of the Indian peninsula in the middle of the third century B.C. He was a truly great king. He conquered his empire by force of arms and ruled it with the sword of the spirit. He became converted to Buddhism and sent missionaries out in many directions. One modern historian says that the name of Asoka shines like a star.

In the seventh century came Allah and his fighting armies. This Moslem invasion was probably the most important event in India's history. Islam, the Moslem faith, is one of the world's greatest religions.

The Moslems were followed in the thirteenth century by two "Princes of Destruction." They were Genghis Khan and Tamerlane, Mongols from China. Their hordes of warriors were ruthless. When they took the city of Delhi, they put all of its eighty thousand defenders to the sword.

In the sixteenth century came the Moguls. The word is a variant of the word Mongol; but this invasion was much later

than the former one. The names of the Mogul rulers are all
well remembered in India. The first of them was Babur, and
the greatest of them was Akbar, who launched many bene-
ficial reforms. Then came Jehangir, who called himself "the
Emperor of the World." His son was Shah Jahan, who built as
a tomb for his beloved wife the most perfect building ever
constructed, the Taj Mahal at Agra. Next was Aurangzeb,
who was the "grave-digger" of the Mogul dynasty. His reign
was full of foreign wars, religious strife, and famines.

THE EUROPEANS ARRIVE

Vasco da Gama, the daring Portuguese explorer, rounded
the Cape of Good Hope and reached Calicut in southwest
India in 1498. He was followed by four centuries of European
occupation, by the Dutch, French, and British. Under the
British the country consisted of two parts: British India and
the India of the 562 native princes. Some of these princely
states were very large, Kashmir for instance; some were very
petty. The Hindu princes were called *maharajas;* the Moslem
princes were either *nawabs* (governors) or *nizams* (rulers).
The highest British official was the viceroy, who lived in
splendid pomp. He was responsible to the secretary of state
for India in London. Britain and its representatives in India
profited greatly by the occupation, but the British civil officials in India were on the whole a very capable and devoted
group of men. Even today in India there are people who wish
they were back again.

INDIA TODAY

India won its freedom from Great Britain in 1947. It became a republic in 1950. Its constitution is like that of the

United States and grants freedom of worship, freedom of press, and freedom of speech. There is universal suffrage. The Prime Minister is now Jawaharlal Nehru, who is in some respects a disciple of Gandhi's. He preached nonviolence for some time, but his prestige as a man of peace was shattered when he violated the Charter of the United Nations by taking the little Portuguese provinces in western India by military force.

PAKISTAN

The dispute with Pakistan over Jammu and Kashmir has been going on ever since 1947. These areas were Moslem by large majorities. By the terms of the partition they should have gone to Pakistan. But the ruler of these states, a Hindu who was at the time fleeing from his rebellious people, ceded his country to India and asked for protection. India immediately dispatched its soldiers. The fighting was stopped by the United Nations, which subsequently recommended a plebiscite to settle the question. But Nehru refused to agree. And there the matter still stands.

Meantime Pakistan, fearing the growing military might of India, seems to be drawing closer to China.

COMMUNIST CHINA

In October, 1962, China invaded India, and the two most populous countries in the world, China with about 669 million people, and India with about 440 million found themselves at war. The United States rushed in military supplies, not wanting to see the most powerful democratic nation in Asia swallowed up by the most powerful communistic nation in Asia. The Chinese subsequently withdrew.

THE GREATEST BATTLE

The most important question for India at the moment is still this: can the government bring its many millions out of the slough of hunger, poverty, and hopelessness into a new day? This does not mean just a showpiece like the great city of Calcutta, which has three million people, jute mills, steel mills, and other factories as well as near-by coal, iron and bauxite. It means the five hundred thousand little villages of mud huts and undernourished cattle and famished peasants. When the Pakistan dispute is at last settled, and the Chinese Communists at last sent home, the people of India will still be there.

India is so large a nation and so important for the future of South Asia that we have asked four of her young people to speak for her. Rajendra Prasad Misra is a Hindu boy living in Benares by the holy Ganges River. Roshmi Roy is a girl who lives in India's largest city, Calcutta. Narayana Murthy is a Telugu boy from Madras. The Telugus are one of the most important groups in southern India. Finally, Tina Vakil is a Parsee girl from Bombay.

I LIVE ON THE HOLY RIVER

by Rajendra Prasad Misra

VARANASI ON THE GANGA

My city was called *Banaras* for a long time by us Indians, and the English called it Benares. But recently our government has gone back to the original name, which was Varanasi. Varanasi lies on the left bank of the Ganges River, which we call the *Ganga*. At one end of the city the little river *Asi* flows into the Ganga and at the other end the river *Varuna* empties into it. So in the old days the people joined the two names and got the name Varanasi for the community.

To us Hindus the Ganga is a very holy river. It was created by the great god Shiva himself. It's the mother river of India. So Varanasi on the banks of the Ganga is the holiest place in the world for Hindus. For more than a thousand years it has been a place of pilgrimage. People used to come on foot, sometimes walking for many months to reach it. They still come by the hundreds of thousands, but now they come in trains and autos and planes.

The left bank of the river, where the city lies, is very steep; and high flights of brick and stone steps have been built on the *ghats,* a word which means steps or banks, so the people can reach the side of the river easily. Men sit on little platforms under big umbrellas and give out colored powders to put on the foreheads of the pilgrims. People come in the dark of the early morning to bathe in the river, to drink of the water, to pray with folded hands, and to watch the sun rise. They bring along brass bowls so they can carry some of the holy water away with them.

All along the ghats, which extend for four miles, there are palaces, big inns where the pilgrims can sleep, and temples. There are sixteen hundred important temples in my city and you couldn't count the little ones.

After the pilgrims have bathed in the river and so purified themselves, they all take some of the river water through the narrow lanes of the city to the Vishwanath Temple. This temple is often called the Golden Temple, because it is topped with a golden dome. When the pilgrims get there they sprinkle the holy water from the Ganga on the statues of the gods and make offerings of flowers. The flowers are usually marigolds, white jasmines, and pink roses.

This temple is the holiest temple in the world to the Hindus.

Hindus believe in cremation and there are two burning ghats on the river where every day dozens of bodies are cremated.

When the flood waters come every year, the level of the river rises thirty to forty feet and spreads over all the low land on the other side of the stream until it's a mile wide. Then many of the stone steps and the smaller temples are completely covered.

A HINDU BOY

I'm a Hindu myself and every morning we have prayers in my home. On Saturday and Sunday, when we have no school, my mother takes me to the river to bathe and then we go together to the Golden Temple with water and flowers for the gods. We take our shoes off and go into the temple barefoot. I worship all the gods, but Shiva is the greatest of them all.

I swim in the Ganga too. I'm a very good swimmer and I've won a prize in that sport. I often swim across the river with other boys and then swim back again. The river is wide here, too.

I go to other temples besides Vishwanath. One of the most interesting is the Monkey Temple. There are many monkeys that stay there all the time. People feed them and sometimes they snatch away the flowers the pilgrims were about to offer to the gods. They scamper all over the buildings. On Tuesdays and Saturdays I often go there.

CALCUTTA

I live in the sacred city now, but I wasn't born here. I was born in Calcutta twelve years ago. My father is dead, but at the time of my birth he worked in a bank in that big city. Then he opened a textile shop in Varanasi. He dealt in the handmade silks for which Varanasi is famous. The silk thread comes from Lucknow, but the cloth is made up here. I was eight when my father died and then the family moved to Varanasi.

During those Calcutta years we lived on two floors of an apartment house in the heart of the city. We had twenty rooms on the fifth and sixth floors. We needed all those rooms, for I have five brothers and three sisters, and two of my father's brothers lived there with their own families. There wasn't any lift in the building, so we had to climb up the stairs. But when we reached our place it was very nice. We had electricity, toilets, and all the other comforts. There were two servants to help with the work.

My oldest brother is now running my father's shop in Varanasi, and my second oldest brother is in the crushed-stone business at Chandal, which is near Calcutta. I'm the youngest in the family.

A PRIVATE TUTOR

I did not go to school at all when we lived in Calcutta, but when I was seven a private tutor began to teach me Hindi. That was all I studied. The rest of the time I was outdoors playing football and cricket, or flying kites. There is a season for kites and we used to try to bring down the other fellows' kites. We had many kite fights.

OUR CAMEL IN JAIPUR

My father was born in Calcutta, but my mother was born in Jaipur, and my father had a good deal of business in that part of India. I belong to a particular large community that came originally from Marwar, which is not far from Jaipur. We are called the *Marwari Hindus*. This community is now scattered all over India and other parts of the world. The men are traders, bankers, and business people.

I have often gone to Jaipur. I've gone for festivals, for family marriages, and just for holidays. They have a big fair in the city and my father was interested in it from a business standpoint. There were a few amusements for the children, but the most fun was in riding the elephants they always had there.

Jaipur is the capital of the province of Rajasthan. It's called the pink city, for many of the houses are built of pink stucco. The city is laid out regularly with wide streets. The whole place belongs to the maharaja there, who is one of the wealthiest native rulers in India. Queen Elizabeth II has visited the maharaja twice. On her latest visit he was the only maharaja she visited. He has a wonderful palace in the center of the city.

The whole country around Jaipur is very dry and sandy and the best way to travel in it is by camel. So my father used to own a camel because of his business interests. My grandfather had to travel too. He used to lend money. I often took long rides with them. The camel was a one-humped camel and could easily carry the three of us.

MY EDUCATION

When I came to Varanasi I was put in school for the first time. I didn't do very well there, however, and at the end of the first year I was taken out and sent to Smith's Nursery and Primary School, which is a private school with about a hundred and forty boys and girls in it. It occupies the old parsonage of St. Paul's Church, which is a Christian church belonging to the Church of India. The school, however, is not connected with the church and is for everybody. There are very few Christians in it. Mrs. W. H. Smith, the headmistress, is an Indian. She used to be a government inspector of schools. Her husband is English and is the manager. Many people think this is the best school in the city. I was admitted in July, 1961, and have been here for two years. I'm doing better in my studies now.

My subjects are: Hindi, Bible, English literature, writing, dictation, grammar, composition, recitation, arithmetic, history, geography, nature study and science, drawing, singing, physical training, and work. Under "work" all the students, even the boys, are taught to sew, and darn, and knit, and to make things of paper.

Of these subjects I like geography the best. I want to go into business like the other members of my family. My brother is thinking of sending me abroad a little later to study, probably in England.

HOW I SPEND THE DAY

I rise at five and have breakfast of milk and biscuits. School begins at seven, and as I live one and a half miles away my brother takes me on his bicycle. For most of the pupils school ends at twelve thirty, but I work with private tutors until five. My brother brings me my lunch, usually *chapaties*, which are pancakes of unleavened bread. Chapaties are sometimes fried in *ghee*, which is purified butter. Then they are called *puries*. At five I go home either in a rickshaw or a bus, or else I walk.

When I get home I go out to play until it's time for dinner at seven. We are vegetarians, though my brother eats meat outside the house. At home for dinner we have chapaties and *dal*, which is a cereal that comes from gram, a good deal of fruit (guavas, plums, oranges, or *musammis*, which are citrus fruits like oranges), and tea or water to drink. I may listen to the radio afterwards for a little while, but I'm usually in bed at eight o'clock. Sometimes, however, I go to the cinema in the evening.

MY BROTHER'S SHOP

We have no school on Saturday or Sunday and then I go to the river and to the temple to worship. I may go out to play too, or I may go to my brother's shop to help there. My brother's shop is in the Bara-Bazaar. This is a little ways from the Ganga and in a district called *Chawk*, which is a place for shops. At the shop I'm trying to learn the business.

I ride a bicycle and I play a drum called the *tabla*. This is a kind of small kettle drum. My brother plays other instruments, and so we play together. I speak Hindi and a little English.

FESTIVALS

Divali is the festival of lights and it lasts for five or six days. It's a very happy time, when every house and every town are ablaze with candles and earthen lamps. We shoot off firecrackers late into the night.

Another big festival is called *Khichri*. It's a harvest festival which comes in June when the dal is ready to be cut. We bathe in the Ganga, go to the Golden Temple, and have special things to eat at home. Rice and dal are mixed and cooked together, and this is called *khichri*. We may make cakes of linseed and pressed rice. But the most exciting thing we boys do is to fly kites. We try to bring down other kites with our kites.

The *Holi Festival* comes in March. Then the people throw colored water on each other and daub red powder on each other's foreheads.

I LIVE IN INDIA'S LARGEST CITY

by Roshmi Roy

LA MARTINIÈRE

The story of my school is associated with the story of an extraordinary Frenchman who died more than a hundred and fifty years ago. His name was Claude Martin and he was born in the Rhone Valley at Lyons, France, in 1735. At the age of sixteen he enlisted in the French army as a common private for service in India. At that time France and England were fighting each other for my country. After a time the French were defeated, and when the British East India Company offered Martin a commission he accepted it on condition he would never have to fight his own people. As the representative of the country at the court of one of the native princes in Lucknow, he became a close friend of this ruler and came to occupy a position of great importance. Through the favor of the ruler and through his own ability as a businessman he accumulated an immense fortune, which amounted to many millions of pounds when he died in 1800. Before his death the East India Company had made him a major general, though this was only an honorary title.

In his will he left most of his money to found three schools, one in Lucknow, one in Calcutta, and one in Lyons, his birthplace in France. Each of these schools was to bear the name *La Martinière*, and he willed that each of them was to teach the English language and the Christian religion. The Calcutta school was established in 1836. And that's how it happens that I am a student at La Martinière in Calcutta.

MY EARLY LIFE IN CALCUTTA

I was born in a nursing home in Calcutta thirteen years ago. The family still lives in the house we occupied then in the southern part of Calcutta. It's a big brick house with three floors on a street corner. My father had two married brothers who live in the same house but in separate apartments. He had two other brothers who lived outside. Beside our house there is a small flower garden.

My father's name is Mihir Roy and my mother's name is Dhara Roy. Both my parents were born in Calcutta, and I am their only child. My father is in the importing business. He imports food, loads it at dockside, and then transports it in trucks wherever he can sell it. The company belonged to one of his uncles and now my father and all his brothers share in it.

I don't remember very much about my early life; but when I was three, my parents sent me to La Martinière, and I've been here ever since. First I went to the nursery school for two years. I had a great deal of fun there, since I played with all kinds of toys. At the school they had slides, swings, and other play equipment. The children all loved to go to nursery school, for there were so many things to do.

MY SCHOOL LIFE

After nursery school I went to lower KG (kindergarten) for a year, and then to upper KG for another year. After that came a year of what we call "transition." Then came the different forms, each for a year: form one B, form one A, then two, three, four, and five. I'm now in form five, and next year I would be in form six, if the government hadn't decided to do away with the forms and call them all classes. So I shall jump next year from form five to class nine. I shall have two more years after that at my school before I'm ready for college. But at that point my father wants to send me abroad instead of continuing my education in India. Probably I'll go to America.

Up to form three the boys and girls are together. Then the boys move across the street to a school of their own, though it's still part of La Martinière. The boys' school has a fine hall, and all important school functions are held there.

Our school is one of the best schools in Calcutta. Some people say it's the very best. We have five hundred fifty girls, and eighty of them are boarders.

I'm studying Hindi, Bengali, English, science, math, history, geography, singing, physical training, drawing, and crafts. In the last are included needlework and knitting. I like my science and drawing best, but later I'd like to go into the I.A.S. (Indian Administrative Service) and work for my government. To enter this service I shall have to pass an examination after I get through college.

We have a playground and a swimming pool at school, and the school is noted for its sports. We have basketball, badminton, tennis, swimming, and tennyquoits. Our school teams play other schools in Calcutta. I'm not on any of the teams, however, and I'm not very fond of sports.

A DAY IN MY LIFE

I get up at six in the summer, but in the winter it's usually a half hour later. Then comes breakfast: eggs, toast, and milk. School begins at eight fifteen, and my father's chauffeur takes me to school, which is about a mile away from my home, in my father's car, called a Hindustan Ambassador. At eight thirty we have a religious service conducted by Miss Laurence, the principal. It's a Christian service with the Lord's Prayer. No one is compelled to go but all the girls do go, though there are very few Christians in the school.

Classes begin at nine and last until one. Then I go home in my father's car for lunch. I have rice, meat or fish, vegetables, and dal. These are all mixed together with the rice. I drink water. When we have school games, they are scheduled for two thirty, but I seldom go back for them. I usually have two or three hours of homework in the afternoon. Then Mummy and I often go out for a drive. Sometimes I listen to the radio, and about twice a month I go to the cinema, though I don't like it very much. We have our dinner at nine thirty. This time we have meat and vegetables and no rice. We eat a flat cake made of flour, which we call *roti*. After dinner I read a little and go to bed about ten thirty.

Saturday we have school in the morning. In the afternoon I do some homework.

On Sunday I often play ping-pong at home with my cousins.

THE ROTARY CLUB

My father was president of his Rotary Club last year, and next year he will probably be governor of his district which is all of eastern India. He travels a great deal to visit other clubs and Mummy and I often go with him. I've traveled in many parts of India, almost everywhere except in the south and in Kashmir.

Two years ago there was a Rotary International meeting in Tokyo and I went with my father and mother. We took a steamer to Chittagong in East Pakistan and then we stopped at Rangoon, Singapore, Hong Kong, and Yokohama, before we got to Tokyo. At each place we were allowed to spend some time ashore. I think I liked Hong Kong the best, and we stayed there for two or three days each way. But I liked Japan also very much. We were in Tokyo for about a week, and then we visited Kobe, Osaka, Kyoto, Nara, and a few other places. I saw Fuji too. We used to stay at the Japanese hotels and slept on the *tatami*, or thick matting, on the floors. I saw the gardens, and pagodas, and temples. Japan is a lovely country.

I'M A HINDU

Two years ago I went to Varanasi on the Ganga and bathed in the river. But when I got to the Golden Temple I would not enter, because it was so dirty. The son of the great god Shiva is the elephant god, and a little image of him is above the main entrance to the temple. People bring water from the river and throw it on this little statue, so that there's always a pool of water just inside the doorway. People come to the temple with bare feet and the streets are very dusty and dirty, so this pool of water gets very muddy and the mud is tracked all over the floor of the temple.

In Calcutta the Temple of Kali is the most famous one, but I've only been there once. We don't have prayers in our home and I don't regularly go to the temples.

MY DRESS

At school we all wear uniforms. We wear one-piece white dresses with white socks and black shoes. On special days we put on the school emblem. I shall not begin to wear Indian dress until I'm about eighteen. Then I'll put on a colored *sari* with a silken *choli*, or blouse. Most Indian women wear many bracelets and rings.

HOLIDAYS

We have five or six days at Easter and the same at Christmas, but we don't celebrate these Christian holidays in any other way. From May to the middle of June we have six weeks vacation and we get three more weeks in September.

Of course, we observe our own festivals. *Dussehra* is one of the most important. In Delhi they burn big effigies of demons which are made of papier-mâché and stuffed with firecrackers. These may be twenty-five or thirty feet high.

We have celebrated January 26th every year since the day in 1950 when India declared itself a republic. Now we have parades and speeches on that day.

CLASSICAL DANCES

I take part in classical dancing. The girls at the school give these dances at special school exercises. The most famous of these dances is called *Bharata Natyam.* It began in the temples and is deeply religious. It takes years to become a really good classical dancer.

LANGUAGES

Bengali is my native tongue, but I speak English too, and I've just begun to study French. I don't know Hindi very well.

I'M A TELUGU BOY

by Narayana Murthy

I LIVE IN MADRAS

I was born in Madras fifteen years ago, and I've lived there all my life. Madras is a big city on the Coromandel Coast in the southeast of India. There is a wonderful beach, called the Marina, which runs for many miles along the Bay of Bengal. It's a very wide sandy beach and a very long one. People say it's one of the finest beaches in the world.

THE FAMILY

My father used to be a kind of sheriff, called a *munsiff*. He went about serving warrants in different villages in Andhra Pradesh, which is just north of Madras Pradesh (Madras State). I used to go with him as he traveled about, sometimes even to the jails. Once, when I was a very little fellow, I wandered away and got lost for two hours.

Before I began to go to school my father left us, and now my mother, my three sisters, and I live alone in two rooms on the second floor of an apartment house, called Edinburgh

House. My two oldest sisters are twins. They are both studying medicine at Madras University, which faces the Marina on the shore. This is their first year there. They want to be doctors, and perhaps have their own nursing home. If they succeed they will name the nursing home for my grandfather, who was an accountant in the government and left money for our education.

My youngest sister, who is thirteen, is a student at Christ Church High School, from which I graduated last year.

THE TELUGUS

I'm a Telugu. I belong to a large community of people who are found in Madras and in the country to the northwest of Madras. There are thirty-three million of us. We speak one of the Dravidian languages, and in this group is included the important language of Tamil, which is spoken all over southern India and northern Ceylon, and about twenty other languages in central and northern India. About ninety million people speak these languages, which come from the ancient Sanskrit.

CHRIST CHURCH HIGH SCHOOL

As a little fellow I used to roll marbles and hoops, skip rope, and play games like ring-around-a-rosy. Then in 1952 I entered Christ Church High School in the first standard. Last year I was in the eleventh standard and I graduated. I got a double promotion once, jumping from the fifth to the seventh standard.

During my last year I studied Tamil, English, math, history, geometry, algebra, and trigonometry. I won distinction in every subject except English. In 1962 I was the Silver Medalist at the school, and two years before that one of my twin sisters was a Silver Medalist. Of my own subjects I liked math the best, and I want to be an electrical engineer.

Last year the National Council of the Y.M.C.A. in India offered a prize of fifty rupees for the best essay on India written by any student in the country. The prize was given by Mr. Robert D. Stern, of Cincinnati, Ohio, the President of the United States Shoe Corporation. I wrote an essay of about twenty pages and won the prize.

Our school was divided into four houses named after English schools: Rugby, Charter, Eton, and Harrod. I was in Harrod. Teams from these houses played against each other and played other schools also. My favorite sports were the long jump and the high jump, and also the hundred-meter and two-hundred-meter dash.

We had monitors who kept order in the classes when the teacher was out, and prefects who made rules, handled questions of discipline for the whole school, and arranged for special functions. I was a monitor in the ninth and tenth standards and prefect in the tenth and eleventh standards. There were about twenty prefects for the whole school.

THE GUANASEKARAN MEMORIAL CLUB

This club is named for a very good man who was a social worker in Madras. It's a club for men, but they have many activities for boys too, and I often go there. In the competitions at the club I came off first in the hundred-meter and two-hundred-meter dashes, and first in junior caroms.

THE VELAN INSTITUTE OF COMMERCE

I'm now taking a six months' course in the Velan Institute, a commercial school which is approved by the government.

After that I will attend the pre-university class for one year, and I've already passed my examinations. Then I'll have four years of professional study before I get my B.E. (Bachelor of Engineering). After that I want to go abroad, to America, if it's possible. I don't yet know whether I can manage this. The money my grandfather left is only for our education in India.

HOW I SPEND THE DAY

I get up at six and after my prayers I have breakfast, consisting of *idlis* and *dosais*. The first is a type of rice and the second is a kind of pancake. I drink coffee. Then I study for a while before starting for the Institute. I only have an hour there for shorthand and typing, and then I'm home for the rest of the day. I practice my shorthand at home, but I can't practice typing there for we have no typewriter.

Lunch comes at twelve and then I take a nap for three hours. At four I have coffee and then I often go for a walk along the sea. My mother doesn't like me to do this for the surf is often very high. A week ago four people were washed away and drowned. I don't swim.

I like to play hockey, football, cricket, and tennyquoits. Indoors I play chess, checkers, and caroms.

I'm home at seven and usually I read for a little while before we have our dinner at eight thirty. Dinner consists of rice, fish, and meat (no beef or pork), vegetables, and water to drink. I'm in bed about nine thirty or ten.

MY RELIGION

Like most of the Telugus, I am a Hindu. At home we have photos of the gods and goddesses, and one statue of Sai Baba, who is our special family god. I pray before them every morning and evening. I usually go to the Parthasarathi Temple, which is dedicated to Vishnu.

The priests give lectures in the temple on Hinduism, and when these lectures are held the boys and girls have to go.

There is a very famous temple in Andhra Pradesh, called *Tirupathi*, a Telugu word meaning "Venerable Lord." Pilgrims from all over the world go there to offer flowers and fruit and burn pieces of camphor on the altar. Women go there to give thanks when their babies are born or when they recover from an illness. This is an important place of pilgrimage, but it's about seventy miles away from Madras and too far away for me to go there often.

We have a good many religious festivals. At *Vinayaka Chathurthi* we go to the shops and buy clay models of this god. At *Sri Krishna Jayanthi* we pray in the temple at midnight. At *Dassera* we pray for all the goddesses.

Divali is a wonderful sight. Lights burn everywhere in the cities and towns. Children set off fireworks and firecrackers.

There are many different sects in Hinduism with many different beliefs and customs. Often particular animals are associated with particular gods: for example Siva always rides on a bull; Vishnu rides on a bird called the *garuda;* and Skanda rides on a peacock.

I've never traveled outside the vicinity of Madras, but I know something about the rest of the world, because I collect stamps, coins, and books.

I'M A PARSEE GIRL

by Tina Vakil

WHO ARE THE PARSEES?

We Parsees came from Persia. The name *Parsee* is just another way of writing Persian. We are followers of Zoroaster,
or Zarathustra, who was a divine prophet in Persia. When the
Arabs conquered Persia in the eighth century, our ancestors
had to choose between Islam and death. The Moslems said to
us, "The Koran or the sword!" We didn't want either the
Koran or the sword. We wanted to live in peace with our
own religion. So many of us fled to India, where we settled on
the coast of Gujarat. The Hindu ruler of this part of India
welcomed us and we have lived here ever since. Now we all
speak the language of this state, which is called *Gujarati*, and
Bombay is the principal center of our faith in India. There are
about a hundred thousand of us.

OUR FAITH

We believe that there are two great forces in the world:
one is light and goodness; the other is darkness and evil. The

symbol of our faith is the divine fire that burns in our temples and is never allowed to go out. This fire was originally brought from Persia. In the temple it burns on an altar in a separate room which we are never allowed to enter. We can see the fire, but only the priests are allowed to go near it. When they do they must cover the lower part of their faces with something like a surgical mask. There are about a dozen priests in my temple, and they keep the fire burning with sandalwood.

The priests are always dressed in white. They are allowed to marry and have families. A boy between the ages of twelve and sixteen who wants to become a priest can enter the service of the temple as a novice. Then when the older priests think he is ready he may become a regular priest.

We believe in *humata, hukhata,* and *huvrashta.* These words mean "good thoughts," "good words," and "good deeds."

OUR RELIGIOUS CUSTOMS

When children are seven or eight there is a thread ceremony for them in the temple. The priests put *sudras* and *kustis* on them. The sudra is a white undershirt, and the kusti is a long cord that contains seventy or eighty woolen threads. The cord is wound around the waist and the sudra and kusti are always worn from this time on. The sudra and kusti, however, must not become frayed. When they begin to show signs of wear, we must buy new ones to take their place.

There are no regular religious services except on special occasions. We pray at sunrise and at sunset and whenever we want we go to the temple to pray. Non-Parsees are not allowed within our temples. Our people have always lived apart. But recently there has been a little intermarriage with people of other religions. A boy who marries a non-Parsee woman may remain a Parsee, but a Parsee girl who marries a non-Parsee boy ceases to be a Parsee. You have to be born a Parsee to be one.

There are other religious customs that are peculiar to us. We do not bury our dead or cremate them. We take them to the Towers of Silence and after a religious service we leave the bodies exposed to be eaten by the vultures. Then for ten days after death there are services in the temple.

New Year's is another day for special celebrations. We all go to the temple on that day, and afterwards we put on new clothes, visit our relations and friends, and have big feasts. However, there are two sects among us and they have different calendars. The older sect that came to India in the eighth century celebrates New Year's on August 31. But the other sect, which we call the Irani, who came to India long after my ancestors did, think that March 21st is the real New Year's.

September 6 is another day of celebration. This is the birthday of Zoroaster. Once again we go to the temple, visit, and feast.

PARSEE CLOTHES

Parsee men wear long white coats, usually fastened in front by two tapes tied in bows, and white trousers. On their heads they wear a hat that looks a little like a derby without a brim. Women wear white *saris*. Young people like me, whether we are girls or boys, usually wear European clothes. But when I dress up I wear a sari just like those that most Indian women wear.

Sometimes poorer men wear dark-colored coats, because they don't show the dirt so much, but white is much more common. It's a symbol of truth and purity, which are the fundamentals of our faith.

MY PARENTS

My father and mother were both born in Bombay. Most Parsees are merchants, or traders, businessmen of some kind. My dad is with the Bombay Dye and Manufacturing Company. His first name is Nash. I was born in a hospital sixteen years ago, but my home has always been in a suburb to the north of Bombay called Bandra. This is about nine miles away from the center of the city. Our house is on a point of land that juts out into the Arabian Sea. The place is called "Land's End," and the house is called *Mon Repos*, which is French for "my rest." It's an apartment house in which four families live, and it faces the west. We get lovely sunsets over the water. This is a residential section and there are other apartment houses near ours. We have about seven rooms.

The shore is rough and rocky here and there is no safe place to swim. There is, however, a little rocky beach which is safe enough to play on, and this is where the little children are usually found. As a small girl, I used to skip rope and play blindman's buff with the other girls. I also played with dolls.

ST. JOSEPH'S CONVENT

This is a Catholic school about a mile away from my home, and Mummy used to go there. So I started in kindergarten there when I was four, and my mother took me in a bus. After a year in kindergarten I went on through eleven standards until I graduated from the school. There were nuns, of course, at the school, but most of the teachers were lay persons.

I'm in the midst of a three months' vacation now and afterwards I shall start in the College of Commerce and Economics, which opens in July. I'll have English, French, civics, Indian public administration, and perhaps other subjects. When I'm through school I want to go to work, and I think I'd like to work for some airline, but on the ground, for my parents don't want me to fly.

I'm not particularly interested in sports, and I don't play any musical instrument, but I do dance. I speak Gujarati, Hindi, and English. At home we speak Gujarati and English.

I haven't traveled much, just to places around Bombay, but I like to know about other lands.

8. KASHMIR

VALE OF THE FLOATING HOUSES

JAMMU AND KASHMIR

Jammu and Kashmir are always grouped together. They are the two districts that make up the big state of Kashmir, over which Pakistan and India have been quarreling ever since partition. Jammu is the southern part of the state, north of East Punjab. It's a region of plains and low hills. Jammu City is the most important community in the south, but it is not very large. The language spoken everywhere in Jammu is *Dogri,* which is a dialect of Hindustani.

To get to Kashmir from Jammu you have to climb or fly over a range of the lordly Himalayas, rising in lonely splendor to heights of sixteen to nineteen thousand feet. Then you descend rapidly into the big valley which is the heart of Kashmir. This is about eighty miles long and thirty miles wide. On all sides of the valley rise the mountains, in the north and northeast the majestic Karakoram range, with some of the Himalayas' mightiest peaks: Godwin Austen, 28,250 feet; Nanga Parbat, 26,660 feet; Rakaposhi, 25,550 feet.

The truce line, established after the fighting between Pakistan and India had stopped, left all of Jammu and the most important part of Kashmir in the hands of India, and on November 17, 1956, India incorporated this area into the Indian Union as its seventh republic.

Jammu and Kashmir together have 84,500 square miles, and a population of about five million, more than three-quarters of whom are Moslems. There are, however, more than a million Hindus, and a good many Christians in the country.

"THE HAPPY HIGHLANDS"

The Kashmir Valley has been known for its beauty through long centuries. When the Mogul emperor Jehangir lay dying, his last words were, "Kashmir and nothing else." The Persian poet Urfi described the vale of Kashmir in these words, "Even the burnt bird regains its feathers in Kashmir." Such was the magic of this happy valley, where green meadows glistened beneath the mountain snows, where jasmine and lilac, apple and apricot and almond hung wreaths of fair colors around the clear, blue lake, where the *hanjies* sang their boatmen's song as they paddled their *shikaras*, and the farmers sang their chorus song, the *Shakri*, as they tilled their fields. This was the gay, happy Kashmir of the past.

"THE VALE IN CHAINS"

Today the people of Pakistan sometimes speak of Kashmir as the "Vale in Chains." They talk about the people who are tortured there by the Indian invaders of what should be their land. These, of course, are exaggerations, unless the words refer to the chains of the spirit and the torture of the mind in those who feel that they are enslaved by an alien rule, representing a small minority of the people.

SRINAGAR

This is the most important community in Kashmir. It lies between the Jhelum River, which flows down through Kashmir and the Punjab to join the Indus in West Pakistan, and Dal Lake, which is five miles long and two and a half miles wide. The lake is fed by springs.

There are beautiful houses and flowering orchards around the lake. The river and lake life of Kashmir, however, centers in the houseboats, which are the floating homes of both the rich and the poor. Some of the houseboats are very large, often a hundred twenty feet long and twenty feet wide. The big ones have large living rooms and dining rooms, two or three bedrooms with sanitary toilets, and a kitchen. The rooms are lavishly furnished. There is usually an open deck with a canvas roof above the cabins. The boats keep moving from place to place, and the rent of the boat includes the rent of the place where the boat is moored, the lighting, and four servants. There is always a small boat, a shikara, to take you ashore when you want.

The houseboats occupied by the poor—and there are many of them—are, of course, much smaller and simpler, but they are mansions compared with the mean and filthy hovels inhabited by many of the people in the city of Srinagar itself. The Kashmir of the tourists is not the Kashmir of the Kashmiris.

ISLANDS AND GARDENS

There are lovely islands in the lake, one called Nehru Park, another the Golden Island, and a third the Silver Island. There are floating gardens too, which can be reached through small canals.

Just outside Srinagar are some wonderful gardens, built by the Mogul emperors, who always added gardens to their palaces wherever they went. The garden nearest to Srinagar is *Chashma Shahi*, meaning the "Royal Spring." A spring of icy water is found there, which is supposed to cure diseases. The garden was laid out by Shah Jahan, who built the Taj Mahal.

Two miles farther away from the city is Nishat Bagh, a name which means "Pleasure Garden." It was built by the brother of one of the empresses. It has ten terraces with water pouring down from one to another in a series of sparkling waterfalls. In the background purple mountains rise, and from the topmost terrace you get a wonderful view of the Dal.

Another garden, two miles farther on, is Shalamar, the Abode of Love. It was built by the Emperor Jehangir for his queen.

FOLK SONGS AND DANCES

Many of the folk songs of the Kashmiris are sad songs. The people who live in this lofty land of majestic scenery sing songs lamenting the miseries and hardships they have suffered during long years of foreign domination. They also find vent for personal sorrow in song, such as, for example, the *Lole*, which is sung by one whose beloved has gone away. Then there is the *Vidakh*, the song of grief sung by a mother who has lost a child in death.

Kashmiris do not dance much. While the many tourists in this lovely land are happy and gay, the Kashmiris themselves are on the whole a sober people. But there are those who dance.

The *Bach Naghma* is always done by a boy who sings as he dances. The *Shamshir* dance is a war dance, which is very popular among some of the more warlike tribes. The young girls dance the *Ruf*. They stand in two rows facing each other, step and sway and clap their hands. Other girls dance the *Hik Chichi*, in which a pair of girls take each other by the hands and whirl around madly.

Azra Shah, a Moslem girl from Srinagar, represents the majority religious group. The mountain resort of Gulmarg, to which her family often went in the summer, has been completely destroyed by an earthquake since she told her story to the author. The earthquake reduced fifty-six villages southeast of Srinagar to heaps of ruins, and flattened two thousand farmhouses. Vichitri Rattan Gupta is a Hindu boy who comes from Jammu in the south.

A MOSLEM GIRL IN KASHMIR
by Azra Shah

MY HOUSE

I was born in Srinagar sixteen years ago, but not in the house we now occupy. Our present house is near the Dal. It's a single house of brick with a roof of wooden shingles. There are eight rooms and we have a big garden where we grow both vegetables and flowers. We need a big house for there are eight people living in it.

My father's name is Syed Ahmah Shah. He was born in Srinagar, but he is now the superintendent of police in Udhanpur, which is more than a hundred miles south of Srinagar. He isn't able to get home very much.

My mother, Salma A. Shah, was born in the place where my father is now stationed. She is now in Srinagar taking care of the family. I have a younger sister, who is eight, and a younger brother, who is one and a half. In addition to these members of my immediate family, my grandmother lives with us, and an uncle, an aunt, and a girl cousin. My uncle is a doctor on the staff of the General Hospital, and my aunt is the principal of the Government Women's College. Altogether we fill the house very well.

MY SCHOOL

My school is just across the Jhelum, about a mile from my home, and it's one of the best schools in the city. We have about six hundred pupils, both boys and girls. The boys and girls are together up through the seventh class. Then the boys go to their own school which is a little distance away. I began my schooling here and I'm now in the tenth class.

My subjects are science (physics and chemistry), history, geography, English, which I've studied from kindergarten, physiology, and hygiene. We have physical training too, and sports like hockey, basketball, netball, and rounders, which is played with a small racket and a ball like a tennis ball. We have school teams and I'm on the hockey team.

I like science best of all, and next year I'm going to the Government Women's College. I'm thinking of becoming a doctor, and to prepare for that I'll have to go to the Medical College of Srinagar after I finish with the Women's College.

THE SCHOOL DAY

I get up at seven and have eggs, toast, and milk for breakfast. I help my mother with the housework and start for school in a bus about nine o'clock. School begins at nine thirty and lasts until three. We have a lunch period from twelve to one, and a servant brings me a hot lunch from home, usually rice and curry. After three in the afternoon we usually have outdoor games for a half hour. Then I go home for tea. My homework takes two or three hours, but I often break it by going for a walk with other girls, or by playing badminton or table tennis.

Dinner comes at eight: rice, vegetables, meat, salad, a sweet, and tea. At ten or ten thirty I'm in bed.

HOLIDAYS

Saturday is a half holiday and in the afternoon we often go for a drive in our Fiat somewhere in the valley. We like to drive around the Dal or hire a boat for a pleasant trip on the quiet waters. The boats are called *shikaras*. They are paddled by a man who sits in the stern. In the middle there is a canopy and under it soft spring cushions where you can recline very comfortably.

In the summer we like best of all to go to Gulmarg, which is twenty-eight miles away. For twenty-five miles there is a good road, but after that you have to walk, or ride a pony, or travel in a jeep. The name *Gulmarg* means "the meadow of flowers." When it's hot in the valley, it's always cool there, for the place is eighty-five hundred feet high. Gulmarg is a big grassy bowl and in the center of it is a flat plain where people play golf or ride horseback. You get lovely views of Nanga Parbat from Gulmarg. One of the highest mountains in the world, *Nanga Parbat* means "naked mountain." There is very good trout fishing not far away from the center, but I don't fish. We often spend our weekends in Gulmarg, going on Saturday and returning on Sunday. There is a big hotel there and a number of small ones, but we always rent a house for the season, and we begin to go about the middle of May. There is a club at Gulmarg to which we belong.

Our long vacation comes in the winter from December 16 to March 1. Then we go south to Jammu and rent a place there. Jammu is a small town where the plains begin, and in the winter it is very much warmer than Srinagar. Most of the government offices are transferred there at that time to escape the cold and snow. I have a good many friends there now.

My father can't come home on weekends, but sometimes he has to come to Srinagar on business, and he tries to get a couple of days off for the special occasions.

FESTIVALS

We are Moslems and so we observe *Ramzan*, the month of fasting. Ramzan is followed by *Id*, which is a very happy festival, coming about the end of February. At the beginning of May comes another Moslem festival, called *Bakri Id*. Bakri means goat, and this is the time when each family tries to sacrifice a goat. The meat is divided up. Some of it goes to relations and friends, and a good deal of it goes to the poor.

School closes for some of the Hindu festivals, but we don't celebrate them.

There are national holidays as well as religious ones. On Mahatma Gandhi's birthday, which comes on October 2, the school children all meet in the stadium. There are parades, music, gymnastics, and speeches.

Pundit Nehru's birthday, November 14, is another holiday, and again we all go to the stadium for special exercises on that day.

HOBBIES AND PASTIMES

On Sundays when I'm home I sometimes go to the movies. Most of them are made in India, but I have enjoyed some of the American movies very much. One of them was Hemingway's *Farewell to Arms;* another was *A Summer Place*. I collect stamps and I keep a scrapbook for things that interest me. School children are sometimes taken by train to visit other parts of India. So I've been to Varanasi (Benares), Calcutta, Madras, and Bombay.

LANGUAGES

In this part of India most people speak Kashmiri, but at home we usually speak Punjabi. In addition to these languages I speak Hindi, Urdu, which is the principal language of West Pakistan, and English. I have a pen-pal in St. Louis, Missouri.

A HINDU BOY IN JAMMU
by Vichitri Rattan Gupta

JAMMU

Jammu City is the most important community in Jammu, but it's not very large. My home is in Rajouri. This small town of about four thousand people is 102 miles by road northwest of Jammu City, not far from West Pakistan. The country is hilly here, but it's still a farming region. Most of the people in Rajouri grow wheat. There is no important river near my town. The farmers get water for irrigation and other purposes from canals. The people speak Dogri, which is a dialect of Hindustani. This language is spoken everywhere in Jammu.

HOME AND FAMILY

My father, Shri Rup Lal, is a lawyer in this small community, and our house is bigger than most of the houses there. It has eleven rooms on two floors. I was born in this house thirteen years ago, and I lived there until a few years ago. I have four older brothers, two older sisters, and one younger sister. Two of my older brothers are married.

When I was small I used to play the games most children

play. I rolled marbles and flew kites. I played *ankh macholi* (hide-and-seek) and *guli-danda* (tip cat). I began to go to school in Rajouri when I was six. I entered the first class; but because I had private tutoring at home, I was able to pass the examinations for the eighth class by the time I was eight or nine. Of course, the lessons are very simple in the early classes.

TO SRINAGAR

I have a married brother who lives in Srinagar. He invited me to stay with him and continue my education in a place where the schools are very much better than they are in Rajouri. So I came to Srinagar and entered the eighth class of the Sri Batap Multilateral Higher Secondary School. They have changed the names and the numbers of the classes in this school. After the eighth class come the first, second, and third classes of the higher secondary education. I am now in section B of the second class.

The school is called a multilateral school because there are four different courses, or streams, from which a boy may choose. There is a medical stream, a nonmedical stream, a commercial stream, and a humanities stream. I'm in the nonmedical stream. I study Hindi, English, general science, math, commercial drawing, and social studies. I get the most fun out of my general science and I want to become an electrical engineer.

All my teaching is in English. The school is free for me; I pay no tuition.

WEEK DAYS

My day begins at six. Breakfast consists of eggs and tea. After eating I study until school time. School is in session from

ten to one and from one thirty to four. I go home for lunch
and eat rice and bread, vegetables, meat, sometimes fish, curds
eaten with either salt or sugar, and sometimes pudding. At
four I'm home for tea with bread and butter. After that I go
out for a game of football or hockey. I'm a bit tired when I
come in, so I lie down for a half hour's nap. Then I do some
more homework before I have my dinner at eight o'clock. This
meal is very much like my lunch. After dinner I listen to the
radio, especially light music and children's programs. I'm in
bed at ten.

Saturday is like any other school day.

SUNDAY

Sunday is different. I'm a Hindu, but I belong to a reform
group. We don't worship the many gods and goddesses of
the Hindu religion, and we don't have a temple. We meet in
a hall, where we have meditation and prayer and singing and
listen to a lecture. We don't have any priests or regular leaders, and we don't have Sunday school classes for boys and
girls.

On Sunday afternoon my brother's family (he has a wife
and two children) and I often take a picnic lunch and go to
visit different places around the Dal and the Jhelum River.
We like to take the bus and visit the lovely Mogul gardens
too.

HOME FOR VACATION

My long vacation lasts from December 24 to the first of
March. Then I take the bus for Jammu City where I change
for another bus that takes me to Rajouri. Once in a while I
take the plane to Jammu City and get the bus from there.

The school gives us assignments to do during vacation, so I can't play all the time; but I am glad to be back with my family, much as I like my school in Srinagar.

MY OTHER INTERESTS

I collect stamps; I like to read stories; and about once a week I go to the movies. There was one American movie I liked very much, called *When Comedy Was King*. I like to travel, but I've had only one chance to get out of Kashmir, when I went to visit my sister. She is a student in a college at Jullendar, which is one of the most important places in East Punjab.

HOLIDAYS AND FESTIVALS

August 14, 1947, was our Independence Day, and every year we commemorate that day. India became a republic on January 26, 1950, and we celebrate that anniversary also.

There are several traditional Hindu festivals that don't mean the same thing to us who belong to the reform movement in Hinduism; but still they are very interesting. *Holi*, which is observed all over northern India, comes in March and marks the return of spring. It's a very boisterous festival when people exchange greetings and sweets, and throw colored powders and squirt colored water on each other. That's a day when we don't go out on the street in our best clothes.

Dussehra comes in October. It lasts for a number of days. The deeds of Rama, who fought the demon Ravana in the sacred book called the *Ramayana*, are retold in plays, recitations, and music.

Divali, which comes in October or November, is a very beautiful festival and a very joyous one. It celebrates the victory of good over evil. At night the people decorate their houses and the streets with candles and lamps and electric lights until the whole countryside is ablaze. Divali comes in October or November.

MY LANGUAGES

I speak Dogri, Hindi, Hindustani, and English and now I'm learning Kashmiri.

9. CEYLON

AN ISLAND NATION

LANKA

The official name of Ceylon is *Lanka*, which means "something splendid." Lanka is a pear-shaped island east of the southern tip of India. There are stepping-stones to the mainland thirty miles away, a chain of shoals, called Adam's Bridge.

The island is about 270 miles long and 140 miles wide. A little larger than West Virginia, it has an area of 25,000 square miles, and a population of 6.7 million.

ADAM'S SECOND EDEN

The island is so beautiful that it is sometimes called Adam's Second Eden. The coasts are flat, but there are mountains in the interior. The highest is Pidurutalagala, 8,281 feet high. Another, called Adam's Peak, is 7,360 feet high. Thousands of pilgrims climb it every year to worship. On the mountain there is a hollow that looks as if some giant had stepped there.

The devout pilgrims call the peak the Mountain of *Sri Pada,* or the Mountain of the Sacred Footprint.

People say that thousands of white and yellow butterflies make their last flight to the summit of Sri Pada just before they die.

There are many mountain streams, but only small boats can travel on them.

In the hot, humid, tropical climate many lovely flowering trees and shrubs blossom. The soft blue of the jacaranda, the orange of the flamboyant acacia, the white and red of the oleander hedges, and many other fragrant growing plants make the isle a paradise for nature lovers. One of the finest tropical gardens in the world, with wonderful orchids and ferns, lies on the outskirts of Kandy in the high interior.

THE LION PEOPLE

About 500 B.C. many people came to Lanka from the valley of the Ganges in northern India. They called themselves *Sihalas,* or "lion people." When they arrived they found another earlier people living there, called *Veddas.* The descendants of the Veddas are still on the island, hunting with bows and arrows, collecting wild honey, and growing yams. But these simple people are fast disappearing.

The Sihalas, or Sinhalese, as they are now called, established their capital at Anuradhapura. In the third century B.C. it was one of the chief centers of Buddhism in all the world. The Sinhalese, who are light-skinned with delicate features, now form about three-quarters of the population. Some time after their arrival, darker-skinned *Tamils* came from southern India. They were mostly Hindus and now form from one-tenth to one-fifth of the population. Sinhalese became the official language of Ceylon in 1961, but the Tamils, who have their own language, do not like this, and they are resisting.

FOREIGN RULE

For almost four and a half centuries Europeans occupied the island. The Portuguese were the first to arrive. They came in the early sixteenth century, attracted by the rich spices that were found there, especially the cinnamon. Then the Dutch drove the Portuguese away, and finally the British ousted the Dutch. In 1948 Ceylon became independent. It was the first British crown colony to become a dominion of the British Commonwealth.

CEYLON TEA, COPRA, RUBBER, FRUITS, TOBACCO

The tea grown on the island is famous, and its culture is the largest of Ceylon's industries. The symmetrical tea bushes are found growing even as high as seven thousand feet in many places. In fact, the best-flavored tea is found above four thousand feet. The British introduced tea in 1840, and today Ceylon is the world's second largest producer of that commodity.

The wealth of the west coast consists of coconuts. The coconut palm has a hundred uses. From the lowest roots to the topmost branches every part is valuable. The dried meat of the coconut itself is called *copra*. This is the most important product, as oil comes from it.

The fine rubber tree from Brazil came to Ceylon in 1876. It became very important during the Second World War and flourishes on the hillsides up to two thousand feet.

There are many varieties of bananas and mangoes. The huge jackfruit, which weighs forty pounds or more, has seeds that are roasted and eaten. The small breadfruit is related to it.

Mangosteens have a white pulp and are delicious. Sometimes they are described as "perfumed snow." There are many papayas, pineapples, oranges, custard apples, and soursops. The last are pear-shaped and are slightly acid to the taste. Then there is the evil-smelling durian with its prickly rind. Many people think the cream-colored flesh is the best of all the fruits; but you have to overlook the smell.

The Tamils in the north grow vast quantities of tobacco, but their land has to be irrigated for it.

FISHERMEN

There are many fishermen, but their boats are usually small, often outrigger canoes. They usually fish at night and in the morning come in to drag their heavily laden nets ashore, as they cry in unison: "Ho-li-ho, ho-li-ha!"

ELEPHANTS

There are many elephants in Ceylon, not just tame ones but wild ones too. It's an extraordinary experience to see the Wannis, a forest people, drive them into great enclosures, or *kraals*. Sometimes two to three thousand men take part in these drives, and it may be three or four months before they have gotten all the beasts inside. There the elephants quickly become tame. You can see them in Ceylon, bathing in the rivers and working in the forests.

THE CITIES

The capital is Colombo on the Indian Ocean, a big city of almost a half million people and the most important port. Within its limits are two freshwater lakes. Colombo was the first settlement of the Portuguese. Jaffna is the capital of the northern province and the second largest city, with eighty-four thousand people. Kandy in the interior was the last capital of the kings of Ceylon, who had been driven away from the coast by the Portuguese. It has a population of about 67,000 people.

BUDDHA'S TOOTH

When the founder of Buddhism died about 480 B.C., his body was cremated. Seven relics were left: his skull, two collar-bones, and four teeth. One of the eye teeth, after many long journeys in the course of which, legend says, numerous miracles took place, was brought to Kandy concealed in the hair of a woman; this was about 300 A.D. A temple was built for it right beside the palace of the last kings of Kandy. This temple is called the *Dalada Maligawa*, the Temple of the Tooth.

The tooth now rests on a golden spiral that rises from a golden lotus. This is contained within a nest of six golden shrines shaped like bells and covered with precious stones. The largest of the shrines is about six feet high. It rises in the center of a small room inside the temple. It is said that the value of the gold and jewels is greater than that of the crown jewels in the Tower of London.

You can visit the shrine every day. When the hour arrives four musicians begin to beat on their drums accompanied by a man playing something like a small oboe. The people crowd into the tiny room where the tooth reposes taking with them little trays of flowers, which the priest places on a table in front of the nest of shrines.

The tooth is said to be two and a half inches long and almost an inch in diameter. No one seems to be astounded by the size of it.

THE ESALA PEREHARA

Esala is the name of the month that falls somewhere in our July and August. *Perehara* means procession.

Once a year there are colorful ceremonies in Kandy, when the tooth is carried through the streets of the city. Tradition has it that the processions have taken place every year since the tooth arrived in Kandy. The ceremonies last for ten days. During the first five days the public takes no part in them. Then for several days there are street parades at nine o'clock in the evening. The boom of a gun announces the procession. First come ten whipcrackers. Their function in the early days was to clear the streets. After them come dancers, clowns, acrobats, and stilt walkers. Drums, cymbals, and trumpets provide the music.

All the temples of Kandy, six or eight of them, are represented, the temple chiefs in rich uniforms, and the priests in their yellow robes. About a hundred elephants march along, all of them covered with embroidered cloths. In the middle is a gorgeous tusker, the biggest of them all. His back is covered with a blanket embroidered in gold and silver; his tusks are sheathed in gold. On his back is the casket containing the tooth. He is flanked on each side by another elephant, and then come more of them, lumbering along four abreast. The dense crowds that line the streets are excited, the dancers are frenzied, the elephant bells jangle, the flags flutter, thousands of torches flare, censers smoke.

There is no longer any king to grace the Esala Perehara, but officials of the government are there wearing ancient costumes, and provincial chiefs parade with forty yards of silk wound around their waists and gold-trimmed umbrellas over their heads.

On the last day the procession comes in the daytime.

Nowhere else in the world is there such a spectacle in honor of a tooth.

Our Sinhalese girl is an enthusiastic member of the Girl Guides. Ramani Witanachchi lives in Colombo and goes to the largest Buddhist girls' school in the country. Our Sinhalese boy is Dudley Nihal Dissanayake, who lives in Kandy. He too is a Buddhist, and, of course, he goes to the Temple of the Tooth.

A COLOMBO GIRL GUIDE

by Ramani Witanachchi

THE LITTLE FRIENDS

I'm a member of the Girl Guides, and I love it. There are many girl guides in Ceylon. The organization is very strong here. Little girls between seven and eleven are allowed to join. We used to call them "Brownies," but now they are called "Little Friends." There's a handbook in Sinhalese, our national language, for the Little Friends. And soon there will be one in Tamil, which is the second most important language for our country. The motto of the Little Friends is "Lend a hand," and they try to help around their homes and schools. But they do other things too. Sometimes they collect bottles for hospitals and food for homes for the old people. One Little Friend, who has to wear braces on both legs and finds it hard to sit or stand for long at one time, spent a whole day selling entrance tickets to a big fair for a children's home. Some of them made toys for children with polio. Others gave a Christmas party for little ones.

The Little Friends greet their guests with what they call their "Grand Howl."

I'M A SECOND-CLASS GUIDE

The Girl Guides have very much the same organization here as in other countries. We have tenderfoot, second-class, and first-class guides. I'm now trying for first-class. I have to pass a good many tests.

All the Guides in Ceylon are connected with schools, and they are all organized into companies. We have two hundred Guides in my school and they are divided into A, B, C, and D Companies. The leader of each company is called a "Guider" or a "Captain." Her assistant is a lieutenant. Each company is divided into patrols under the direction of patrol leaders. The captains and the lieutenants have to take training programs.

We all wear white one-piece dresses with two breast pockets and a knotted tie, the color of which depends on the school. Mine is blue. On our ties we wear the trefoil, which is the symbol of our organization. It has two stars on it and the motto "Be Prepared." At our school we have Guide meetings every Friday afternoon.

GIRL GUIDE ACTIVITIES

We have many activities. Camping is important, though girls here don't camp in the open under tents as much as boys do. I have been camping in a house at Ja-ela just north of Colombo, and I had a wonderful time. Ja-ela isn't far from the shore, but we didn't go swimming. Swimming is often dangerous on the west coast of Ceylon. There are many drownings. The east coast of our big island is much safer.

Another activity of ours is called Thinking Day. This

always comes on February 22nd. The main purpose is to re-member Lord and Lady Baden-Powell, who started the Boy Scouts and the Girl Guides. Lord Baden-Powell is dead now, but Lady Baden-Powell came out to see us in Ceylon in 1962. On Thinking Day we have parades, and speeches, and games, and we always try to remember the Baden-Powells.

Social service is also very important to us. The Guides do many different things. The Guides in my school make a spe-cialty of entertaining children in orphanages. There are five or six orphanages in Colombo, and we go quite often to give the children a good time. Other Guides are helping in the *Grow More Food* Campaign. We have raised funds for the deaf and the blind. We have visited homes to help mothers keep their children and their houses clean. We have planted gardens to beautify towns, and we have done many other things.

Our whole program may be described as fun and laughter, work and service.

INTRODUCING ME

I was born fifteen years ago in Galle, on the southwestern shore of Ceylon. It's a rather large place that depends on its fishing. There are many fishermen, but their boats are small. It was in Galle that the Portuguese first landed in Ceylon, when they discovered the country many years ago, but soon afterwards they moved to Colombo. My mother was born in Galle, but my father was born in another town just to the north. It's called Baddagama.

My father's name is Albert. He's a divisional revenue officer for the government, and he is always being sent to various parts of the country. I have two sisters and one brother, all of whom are younger than I.

COLOMBO

When I was three, the family sent me to Colombo to live with my grandmother, so I could go to a good school. I don't remember my early days in Galle, but I know the place very well, since we still go back frequently to visit my uncles, aunts, and cousins there. My grandmother is still living in Colombo.

VISAKHA COLLEGE

My first school was a nursery school, but I was there for only one year. Ever since then I've been going to the Visakha Vidyalaya. The last word means "college." This is the largest Buddhist girls' school in Colombo with three thousand girls. It's very convenient for me, for I live only a few yards away in a single brick house of six rooms with a very small garden attached to it.

I started here in the lower kindergarten, and I've been here for eleven years now, passing through standards two, three, four, and five, then the first, second, and third forms. After that I had to choose between the sciences and the arts; I chose arts. Then came the senior prep and the senior classes. I'm in the senior class now, with two more years to go here. These are called high school certificate I and II. When I finish these classes I want to go to the university, where I might specialize in English.

At the moment I'm taking Sinhalese, which is my mother tongue, English and English literature, Buddhism, math, geography, history, and civics. I like geography best.

I HAVE A VERY BUSY DAY

I get up at six and have breakfast consisting of rice flour mixed with coconut milk or water, to which meat or fish is added. I may eat bread too and I drink either milk or tea. Then I clean my room and say my prayers.

School begins at eight thirty and at ten thirty we have a five-minute break when I get something to drink. From twelve thirty to one thirty I go home for lunch: rice, vegetables, meat, a green salad, fruit, a sweet, and tea. Then classes continue until three. If there are school activities, such as Oriental dancing, elocution, or guiding, they come after that. Then I go home and relax a bit. I may read or go to visit my friends. Our eight o'clock dinner is very much like our lunch. I'm in bed at nine.

TIME OUT FOR FUN

There's no school on Saturday or Sunday. My father has a Skoda automobile and the whole family often goes on picnics and gets dinner somewhere. I am learning how to drive myself, and when I'm eighteen I can get a license.

We play games at home: ping-pong and table games like draughts (checkers), snakes and ladders, monopoly, caroms, and card games.

Our long vacation comes from April 10 to the middle of May. My father gets off then and we often go back to Galle, or to the old Sinhalese capital at Anuradhapura, where there are very large ruins of an ancient civilization. This city has a famous Bodi tree in it. It was under a Bodi tree at Bodh-daya in India that Buddha found the truth, and the tree at Anuradhapura is said to have grown from a slip of that tree. It's over a thousand years old.

Sometimes we all go on what we call a "mad trip." We start out without knowing where we are going. Usually we come back the same day, because we can't find any place to stay overnight.

VAJIRA RAMAYA

Near my school is the Buddhist monastery and temple to which I sometimes go; it is called *Vajira Ramaya*. Buddhists don't believe that you have to go to church every week, and I don't go regularly. But every night I sit up in my bed and say my prayers. On Monday and Friday the priests come to the school to preach to the girls.

A BOY FROM KANDY

by Dudley Nihal Dissanayake

THE CREMATION OF THE CHIEF PRIEST

Today has been a sad day for us Buddhists of Kandy. This afternoon the Chief Priest for this whole district was cremated. He had charge of fifty temples, and he was a very wise, good man. The people gave the money for the funeral and thousands of people took part in it. They carried pictures of the priest and banners that praised him. The streets through which the procession passed were decorated with many long strings of pennants, pictures of the priest, and the yellow banners of Buddhism. At the head of the procession was a long column of men, women, and children, almost all dressed in white. Then came about a hundred men in two long lines pulling the carriage on which the casket was placed with ropes. After the casket came about three hundred Buddhist priests in their yellow robes, many of them carrying black umbrellas.

The procession walked very slowly for a mile and a half out of the town to the place near a cemetery where cremations take place. For the last half mile the road was decorated with palm leaves on each side. For the cremation a tall structure had been built about fifty feet high. It was made of bamboo poles tied together with rope and wound around with white cloth. The big pile of logs underneath was also hidden by white cloths.

There were many speeches and Buddhist ceremonies, before the casket was placed in the middle of the logs and the fire lighted.

BUDDHISM IN MY LIFE

As you can imagine from what I've already told you, I am a Buddhist, and Buddhism is the most important thing in my life. Every day I have prayers at home. About twice a month I go to the Temple of the Tooth, which is my temple. I used to go there every Sunday to get instruction in Buddhism from the priests. And, of course, I see the Esala Perehara.

MY SCHOOL

I don't go to a Buddhist school, however; I go to a Christian college, which was founded by the British about 1820. This was soon after they had conquered the Kandyan kings in 1815. Although the school, called Trinity College, was established by the Church Missionary Society of England, it's not a sectarian school. The principal and almost all the teachers are Ceylonese. There is a regular chapel service with readings from the Bible and the Lord's Prayer, but it's not compulsory and the non-Christian boys don't go. In the senior class I shall have an hour or two every week for the study of Buddhism.

There are twelve hundred boys in my school and we all pay thirty rupees (about six dollars) a month for tuition. In addition to the day pupils there are about three hundred boarders. I was a boarder myself for a year in third standard.

I went to a nursery school near my home when I was five. A year later I changed to my present school, spent two years in kindergarten, and then went through the standards to the forms. I'm now in the fourth form, where I'm taking Sinhalese (the national language), English, Latin, and applied mathematics, chemistry and physics. This year I had to choose between the arts and the sciences. I chose the sciences, for I want to be an engineer.

MY PEOPLE

I was born in a Kandy nursing home fourteen years ago, and I live now in the house where my family lived at that time. It's a modern brick house of seven rooms, only about a mile from my school, so I can easily travel back and forth on my bicycle.

My father's name is Andrew. He was born in Kotmole about twenty miles away, and my mother was born there too. For some years now my father has had a hotel in the heart of the city. It's called the Silverdale Hotel, and it's for Sinhalese people rather than for foreigners.

I have three brothers and three sisters, and I'm the fifth in the family. The oldest of the children is a sister who is studying at the University of Ceylon just outside of Kandy. She wants to be a teacher, I think. An older brother is studying law in Colombo.

MY WAKING LIFE

I rise at six and for breakfast have *aappes,* which the British call "hoppers." This is something like pancakes except that they are cooked in a bowl so that the edges turn up and are thin and crisp. In the middle the aappes are thicker and softer. Sometimes I have cereal too, and I always have fruit and milk.

School lasts from eight to three. The luncheon period is from twelve to one, and my father sends me something from his hotel. I always have two hard-boiled eggs and usually some sandwiches. I have water to drink.

After school I go home and change my clothes. At school I wear a uniform which consists of blue shorts and a white shirt. Next year I'll go into long pants. There's a school badge which you can wear if you want to, but I don't own one. I take off this uniform and get into sports clothes for the athletics which come in the afternoon at the school. From January through March we have cricket, high jump, broad jump, pole vaulting, running, and javelin. April is a holiday month. From May to July we have rugby, and August is a holiday. From September through November we play hockey, and then comes our December holiday. The school has teams that play other schools. I am on the hockey team.

I go home at five forty-five and study from six to eight. Then we have dinner: rice and curry, meat and fish and vegetables, all mixed together. We have a green salad and fruit such as pineapples, bananas, and mangoes. I drink water. I listen to the radio sometimes and read before I go to bed at nine thirty. I like novels, and I'm very fond of the books of Enid Blyton.

HOLIDAYS

On Saturday and Sunday I play cricket and take bicycle rides with other boys. One of the high mountains in Ceylon is Hantanne. It's only a mile or two away and I have been to the top of it. It's about eight thousand feet high. I don't go away for my long vacations, and I've never been out of Ceylon. I've visited the old capital of Anuradhapura, however.

10. AFGHANISTAN

LAND OF THE PERSIAN LAMBS

BETWEEN THE LION AND THE BEAR

For a long time Afghanistan was a buffer state between the British lion and the Russian bear. Russia bordered it on the north for about fifteen hundred miles. Russia's most southerly town, Kushka, lies just outside Afghanistan's northwest corner. The nomadic tribe, the Kirghiz, whose members speak a language closely akin to Turkish, is found not only in northern Afghanistan, but also in southern Russia and western China. It pays little attention to boundaries as it seeks pasturage for its yaks. Some of these people have ceased to wander, because there is good grazing the year round on the Pamir Plateau among the high mountains in the Soviet Union and Afghanistan. It isn't strange that the big bear of the north has had for centuries a profound interest in Afghanistan.

Great Britain has had a similar interest, for until Pakistan was set up as a separate state in 1947 Afghanistan bordered on India, which was ruled by Britain. The Khyber Pass between the two countries has always been the chief invasion route for ambitious soldiers of fortune in the west who wished to extend their conquests into India. Great Britain also was worried for fear Afghanistan might fall into the wrong hands.

THE AFGHAN LEAF

If you look at the map you will see that up in the northeast of Afghanistan there is a narrow strip of land lying between the Soviet Union and Pakistan that reaches for about three hundred miles to the frontier of Sinkiang Province in China. This looks like the stem of the Afghan leaf. It was the route by which Marco Polo, the daring Venetian explorer of the thirteenth century, reached China. Later it became the great caravan route between the Occident and the Orient. This was the famous Silk Route by which the lovely fabrics of the Orient came to the west. It was also the Pilgrim Route by which Buddhism was carried into China. It was the invasion route for the Chinese. Genghis Khan led his Mongol hordes through this gateway into southern Asia. Baber, in whose veins the blood of Genghis Khan flowed, entered by the same rough road to establish the line of Mogul emperors.

Today this strip of land is called the Wakhan. At the western end of it is Zarkhan, which is known as the "place where the salt ends." The people of Wakhan have lived for centuries without salt.

BAMIAN

Bamian in the north central part of Afghanistan was an important center of Buddhist worship. For eight centuries a community of monks lived there. Two gigantic statues of Buddha, hewn out of the high cliffs, still dominate the valley. One of them is 135 feet high, the other 100 feet high. Bamian was on the route to the Orient, and the Buddhist monks who set off to convert the Chinese may very well have started here. In any case, when Genghis Khan swept in from China through the Wakhan, he sacked the whole city.

AN INLAND NATION

Afghanistan has no seacoast. On the east and south it is bounded by China (where the little finger of the Wakhan reaches out to touch it) and West Pakistan. On the west it is bounded by Iran. It has an area of 250,000 square miles and a population of about 13.8 million. The country stretches from the Hindu Kush mountains in the northeast to the western deserts of Helmand. The Hindu Kush are an extension of the Himalayas. The ranges run from the northeast to the southwest. The highest peak is Ter Ajmir, 25,400 feet high. A mountain range in the south shuts off the cool, moist breeze from the sea, and the climate is very hot and dry. Although there are great stretches of desert in the south and west, many fertile valleys and plains lie among the mountains.

FORBIDDEN LAND

It was impossible to reach Afghanistan by sea, and until recently it was impossible to reach it by land. Afghanistan, like Nepal, was closed to all foreigners. There was a sign in the Khyber Pass that read, "It is absolutely forbidden to cross this frontier into Afghan territory." Things have changed now, and the present king is eager to welcome visitors, especially if they can help him modernize his country and build its economy. The king, whose name is Mohammed Zahir Shah, has a title, *Almutawakal Allalah*, which means "He Who Puts His Trust in the Lord."

THE PEOPLE OF THE LAND

Sixty per cent of the people are Pakhtoons who speak Pashto, or Pushtu. The second main language is Persian, which is here called Farsi. But there are many different tribes living in the lonely valleys, all of them jealous of their independence. Most of the people are agricultural or pastoral. But about two million of them are nomads, such as those we have already seen in the north, living in their conical, felt tents, which they call *yurts*, cooking their meals over yak dung fires, and driving their animals from one good pasturage to another.

The people have large flocks of sheep, and the chief export of the country are the lambskins, with their tight curls, ranging in color from gray and golden brown to a deep glistening black. This is *karakul*, commonly called (or miscalled) Persian lamb; I say "miscalled" because its home is Afghanistan, not Persia. It's rather hard to find this skin in Persia, or Iran, today.

There are many camels in Afghanistan. In fact the two-humped, or Bactrian, camel gets its name from the ancient region of Bactria in northern Afghanistan.

There are no pigs in the country, because almost everybody is a Moslem and believes that pork is unclean. So mutton is the meat that feeds the Afghan today. The fat from the tails of the sheep, which are the broadtail sheep, is often used in place of butter.

KABUL AND KANDAHAR

If you enter Afghanistan from Peshawar in Western Pakistan today you drive over the Khyber Pass in a bus or in an auto. You may want to spend the night at Nimla. That's what the Mogul emperors used to do. Shah Jahan had a garden near by. The next day you reach Kabul, the capital (pronounced "cobble"). The city has 300,000 people in it, and the Kabul River flows through the center of it on its way to join the Indus in West Pakistan.

Kabul seems to be, at least outwardly, a man's town. Most of the women, when you see them on the street, wear long robes, which cover their bodies from the crown of their heads to their heels. Over the face falls a portion of this garment, which has a little window in it for the eyes, covered with a kind of coarse mosquito net. The robes may be green, gray, brown, blue, or black. Below the waist they are open in front, and the wind often sends the loose folds blowing out behind. It's a bit amusing to see under these sombre garments gay, flowered knee-length dresses and nylon stockings. Here is a blend of the modern and the traditional.

The streets of Kabul are full of donkeys, soft-lipped camels, and *tongas*, which are two-wheeled carriages drawn by horses. But there are also autos, buses, and trucks. The trucks are often highly decorated with scenes from foreign lands painted on the panels. Just outside Kabul is the tomb of Baber. Kabul's most modern sports park is close by, with a swimming pool and tennis courts. This is perhaps appropriate, for the philosophy of this Mogul emperor was, "Enjoy life freely, O Baber, for none enjoys it twice."

The second largest city is Kandahar, which has a population of 80,000 people. It's a bustling market for dried fruits, embroideries, rugs, jackets, cotton, and imported soaps.

There is little industry in Afghanistan, and the land is certainly one of the less developed nations.

HISTORY

The ancient history of Afghanistan is very much like that of West Pakistan. It's the story of the same invaders, Alexander the Great, Asoka, the Mongols, the Moguls, and the rival western powers. The country became independent in 1919.

Zia Ullah Shirzada is the son of an Afghan general. Rohafza and Rohliga Feroz are very interesting and lovable twins, the first twins to tell us of their lives in this series of books on the *Young People of the World*.

I LIVE IN KABUL
by Zia Ullah Shirzada

OUR KABUL HOUSE

I was born in Kabul fifteen years ago, in the same house
where I now live. It's a brick house near the Kabul River in
the center of the city. We have about eight rooms on one floor.
The roof is made of wood covered with mud. We have a nice
flower garden, and there are peach trees, apple trees, and grape
vines growing in it.

JALALABAD

My father, Taj Mohammed, is a brigadier general in the
Afghan army. He is in the infantry and is stationed at Jalalabad
in the old eastern province of the country. Jalalabad is a pleasant place in the winter for many people who can afford to leave
Kabul when it's cold. The government is building a big dam,
called the Daronta Dam, on the river there. They will have a
power plant to produce 11,000 kilowatts of electricity, and
the Nangarhal Canal will take water from the Kabul River
and irrigate many square miles of desert to the south of the

river. The canal will be fifty miles long, and before all the work is done they will have to build new roads, bridges, tunnels, and siphons.

I have two brothers. The oldest is a year older than I am. My sister, who is the youngest in the family, is nine. My father and mother were both born in Kabul.

MY EARLY YEARS

Boys and girls play games like hide-and-seek when they are little. Later the boys begin to play rougher games like football and putting a shot. Most children learn the folk dances of the people too, and I know the dances that are common in Kabul and vicinity. When we dance on special occasions, like the national or Moslem holidays, I wear our national costume. I have white trousers and a white shirt that is embroidered over the chest. On top of that I wear a vest of heavy cloth which is richly embroidered on the back.

HABIBIA COLLEGE

When I was six I first went to school, a public primary school near my home, where I went for four years. Then I entered Habibia College. This school, named for a former king, was established by the king's son in memory of his father. It takes students from the first grade to the twelfth. I entered the fifth class and I'm now in the tenth.

I have Pushtu, Farsi, English, history, geography, physics, chemistry, geology, and theology. I like theology best and I want to devote my life to the service of my country. Maybe I'll follow in my father's footsteps and enter the army. My father has always been a foot soldier.

THE DAILY ROUND

When school is in session I get up at six. I have eggs, bread, and milk for breakfast. It takes me fifteen minutes to reach the college on my bike and classes begin at eight. School ends at one twenty. There are no afternoon classes, so I go home for a lunch of rice and meat curry, vegetables, and tea. Then I rest for a while before I turn to my homework, which takes about an hour and a half. The rest of the afternoon I am outdoors, usually playing football with the other boys. The school has teams that play other schools and I am on the children's football team.

At six I go home for a glass of milk and a piece of bread, and then I chat with my family and listen to the radio. About twice a week I go to the movies. We have dinner at eight and this is just like our lunch. Then I go to bed at nine thirty.

My father comes home once a week for Thursday and Friday, returning to Jalalabad on Saturday.

PICNICS

I have school on Saturday and Sunday, but Friday is a holiday. Then the family always goes on a picnic. We have a jeep with a four-wheel drive and we all pile into the car and go off for the day. We have favorite places where we like to go. About thirty miles northwest of Kabul is a town on a mountainside called Istalif. Near the town you can get a wonderful view of the Hindu Kush Mountains, and in the town there are beautiful gardens. The people make blue pottery and weave cotton prayer rugs.

Kargha is another place we like. It has a good cafeteria and a dam and a place to swim. I don't know how to swim, but we hire a motor boat.

Paghman is another lovely place. It used to be the King's private estate, but now he has opened it to the public.

Then there's Targi-Gharu, which is the gorge through which the Kabul River flows. The scenery there is very wild.

THE LONG VACATION

The long vacation comes in October, November, and December. I spend the whole of this vacation with my father at Jalalabad, where I have a lot of fun. Besides playing, I also read the books I'm going to have the next year, though the school doesn't ask us to do this.

SPECIAL DAYS

We always celebrate Independence Day, which is really a three-day holiday. Then we celebrate the King's birthday. These are days for parades and bands, speeches and games.

ISLAM

We are Moslems and we fast during *Ramadan* and then feast on the three-day holiday of *Id Fetr*, which comes immediately afterwards, and on the four-day holiday of *Id Adha*, which comes some weeks later. Then almost every family kills a goat or a sheep and gives away most of the meat to relations and friends and the poor. We all get new clothes. They may be European clothes or they may be our special national costume. It's our custom then to go about and visit the people we know, and there are always good things for us to eat.

HOBBIES

I collect stamps and post cards of scenery. I have traveled to a good many places in Afghanistan. I've been up on the high plateau in the northeast, which we call the Pamir, and I have seen the Amu River, which flows into Russia. I fish a little and sometimes I hunt for birds. I speak Pushtu, Farsi, and a little English.

WE ARE TWIN GIRLS
by Rohafza and Rohliga Feroz

NAMES AND NICKNAMES

My name is Rohafza and my sister's name is Rohliga. We are twins and there is no reason why I should be telling our story except that I was born a few minutes before my sister. That makes me the older, of course. It is often the custom in my country for the grandfather to name the grandchildren, and my father's father decided to call us for two famous queens in Afghanistan. *Rohafza* means the "inspirer," and *Rohliga* means the "perfect soul."

We have middle names too, but these are really nicknames. My middle name is *Mina*, which means "a glass of wine." Rohliga's middle name is *Laila*, which means "sweetheart." At school we are always called Rohafza and Rohliga, but at home and among our friends we are always Mina and Laila.

So far as our parents know there were no twins in the family before we came.

We were born in the year 1342, according to the Moslem calendar. In the Christian calendar that would be 1949. The

month was August, but it's difficult for me to figure out what
the day would be in the Christian calendar.

OUR HOMES

We were living then on the other side of the city. When we
were three, we moved to our present house which is only two
blocks away from the Kabul River. In my country we have
three important river systems. One of them flows into the Amu
River which empties into Lake Aral in the Soviet Union. Another disappears in lakes and marshes on the Afghan frontier.
The waters of the Kabul are the only ones that reach the ocean.
This river runs through narrow gorges into West Pakistan
and joins the Indus River, which empties into the Arabian Sea.

Our present house is fairly big and we have a large yard
which is good for all the children to play in.

TARZAN, MULLAH, SHAHBOBO

We are the only girls in the family. We have six brothers.
Our nine-year-old brother is nicknamed "Tarzan" because
Daddy thinks he can climb better than Tarzan. Our youngest
brother is only two. We call him Mullah, which means "priest,"
because he is very serious and very good. When Daddy gets
ready to go out in the morning, Mullah always brings him his
shoes and anything else he needs. He can't talk yet, but he
knows how to get what he wants. If he's hungry he cries. If
he wants Daddy to give him something he tugs at his trousers.
Then our father may give him some little thing, but he always
wants two of everything. So he'll shake Daddy's pants again.
Then when he gets two pencils or two small coins, he goes
around and shows them proudly to everyone. It's a little game
that they play together.

Mamma's nickname is *Shahbobo,* which means "queen of all mothers." Everybody calls her that in and out of the family. This has become her middle name.

MY FATHER IS A HAJI

When my father was about fourteen years old, his father and his grandparents took him to Mecca to make the pilgrimage that all Moslems want to make once in a lifetime. They traveled by boat and during those thirteen days Daddy learned to speak Urdu, which is the language of West Pakistan. Now, since he has gone to Mecca, he is a *Haji,* and he writes his name H. Mohammed Muhsin Feroz. The "H" stands for Haji. He can wear a green turban, too, if he wants to.

Daddy is now a specialist translator in the political section of the United States Embassy. He speaks English and Arabic very well, and, of course, the two languages of Afghanistan, Pushtu and Persian. We call the last of these languages Farsi. He has had this job for four years. Before that he was connected with the team of educators from Columbia University working with the Ministry of Education. For four years he translated and prepared material for them. Previously he was chief of the Bakhter News Agency and editor of the *Daily Islah,* which was a government newspaper.

EARLY LIFE

We were both very frail at first. Our hearts were weak, but Daddy was very careful about the food we ate. The doctors thought that I would have to have an operation because of a small deformity in my hands and feet. But Daddy didn't think so, and he was right. We are both now in excellent physical condition.

ZENEB-E-HOTEKI SCHOOL

We are now going to this school, which is one of the most important public schools of the city. Zeneb was a heroine in Afghanistan history; she belonged to the Hoteki tribe. We are now in the fifth class, studying Farsi, Pushtu, math, reading, history, geography, general science, and theology. We haven't begun to study English yet. I like history, geography, and Pushtu best and I'd like to be a teacher. I am good in my studies. Laila is in the same class with me but not in the same group or room. She likes languages best and maybe she'll be a writer later. She likes to sing and dance and paint. She's very artistic.

There are other differences between us. Daddy says that Laila is more mischievous than I and more of a tomboy. The only thing she's afraid of is lightning. She wants Daddy to buy her a horse, because some of the American girls have horses. I'm more timid than she is, and I want to be a good woman and have a family. Laila always wears trousers, but I like skirts.

THE SCHOOL DAY

Daddy says Laila's lazy in the morning, because she doesn't want to get up at six thirty. Then, he says, I'm lazy in the evening. I try to make Daddy happy in the morning and Laila tries to make him happy in the evening. We both have to help Shahbobo with the housework, for there are ten of us in the family.

For breakfast we have bread and butter, milk and tea, and sometimes eggs. We often have meat or porridge in the morning also. School runs from eight to twelve thirty. Other children have school in the afternoon, but we don't have to go then. For lunch we have rice, curry, meat or chicken or fish, pudding, and water. Then after lunch we have a cup of tea. Daddy wants us to lie down and rest for a bit after lunch, but we don't like to do this. Our homework takes us about an hour, and the rest of the time we play with each other.

In the corner of our yard Daddy has built a big wooden playhouse for us children. It stands on the top of a flight of about ten concrete steps. We always had many toys to play with from the time we were very small.

Dinner is at seven or eight.

HOLIDAYS

We have no school on Friday or Sunday, and the Embassy is closed then too. We often go to Paghman, where there is a public garden with places for games and swimming. We go to the cinema about twice a week, but always with our parents. The stores are open on Sunday, and that is the day we may do a good deal of our shopping.

VACATIONS

Our long vacation comes during the winter from October 15 to the middle of December. Then we often go down to Jalalabad, where it is much warmer than at Kabul. Daddy has bought a small piece of land there and he's planning to build a house when he can.

ISLAM

We are Moslems and we have prayers and ablutions five times a day in our house. But we have a picture of the Madonna on our walls. Daddy says that no one can be a good Moslem unless he believes that Jesus was a divine teacher. The Koran always speaks of "Jesus, the son of Mary." That's why we have a picture of the Christ child and his mother in our home.

II. IRAN

LAND OF THE KING OF KINGS

THE IRANIAN PLATEAU

Between the Indus River in West Pakistan and the Tigris River in Iraq lies the great Iranian Plateau. The western and larger part of it is occupied by Iran, which was called Persia until 1935. Iran is bounded on the north by the Caspian Sea and the Soviet Union, on the east by Afghanistan and Pakistan, on the south by the Gulf of Oman and the Persian Gulf, and on the west by Iraq and Turkey. The country has an area of 628,000 square miles and a population of about twenty-one million people.

In the north are the Elburz Mountains which run east and west across the land just south of the Caspian Sea. The highest of these mountains is Demavend, which rises to 18,550 feet. It's a stately background for the capital city, Tehran. Another chain of mountains, the Zagros, extends from the border of Turkey in the northwest all along the boundary of Iran to Pakistan in the southeast.

THE GOLDEN AGE

The history of Iran goes back for long millenniums. This was due in part to Iran's favored position. The Iranian Plateau is completely surrounded by mountains. Long ago while Europe was covered with deep ice as far south as the Alps, Iran enjoyed a temperate climate. So the plateau was one of the first regions in the world to be cultivated. In those days great forests clothed the southern slopes of the mountains. The people were cave dwellers who lived by hunting and fishing. In the center of the land was a low area filled by an inland sea. Gradually this sea dried up, leaving wastes of sand and salt, which look like fields of snow from the air. As the sea disappeared the people came down from the mountains to the lower plains. Where the old sea lay there are now a number of oases, which get their water from springs and streams. But much of the country is desert and only 8 per cent of the land is now cultivated.

In the fifth millennium B.C. a very high culture existed near Kashan in the center of the country. The archaeologists have been digging near by at Sialk where they have found the ruins of an ancient civilization. They have not unearthed any weapons, so there were probably no wars. Nor is there any evidence of slavery or social castes. It must have been a kind of golden age.

GREAT NAMES

The Persians probably came into the land through the passes of the Caucasus and to the east of the Caspian Sea in the ninth century B.C. There were two principal tribes: the Medes set-

tled in the northwest, and the Persians went farther on and
built their villages in the Zagros Mountains. These two tribes
became very strong. With the Babylonians and the Scythians,
they conquered Assyria in 612 B.C. and destroyed Nineveh,
the capital city. The leader of this victorious army was Cyrus
the Great. He established a mighty empire. It was he who de-
livered the Jews from their captivity. It was he who helped
them to restore Jerusalem and to rebuild the temple there.

The next great name was Darius. His Persian name was
Darayavaush. He was also a great conqueror, a great organ-
izer, a patron of the arts, who built wonderful palaces on high
terraces. His empire was the greatest in the world of his day.
He wrote a letter to the kings who were to succeed him: "This
is my kingdom," he said, "a land of brave men and beautiful
horses. May Ahuramazda [the chief spirit for good in the
Persian religion] keep it under his protection for evermore.
O Thou, who rulest after me as king over this land, if thou
wishest to keep it lasting and prosperous, avoid falsehood and
mete out punishment to the liar. Be benevolent, forbearing, and
just."

Darius had two capitals. His permanent capital, which was
at Susa, near the modern Dizful, is called Shushan in the Bible.
You can read about it in the books of Esther and Daniel. Darius
built a magnificent palace there, which he occupied in the
winter. He built also a Royal Way from Susa to the Aegean
Sea, which extended for 1,666 miles. The king's messengers
traveled on horseback. Their speed was said to equal the speed
of a crane in flight.

In the hot weather the king moved to Persepolis, a city built
on the plateau about 500 B.C. Its name meant the "city of

Persia." There were thousands of Persian noblemen and the court ceremonials were dazzling in their splendor. The palace was burned when Alexander came from the west, but the ruins of Persepolis remain. Some think they are the finest ruins in the world.

Darius was greatly interested in his people. He built many irrigation canals, mostly underground, and he tried to educate the illiterate.

Other famous names appear in the varied history of this great country. Xerxes I, the son of Darius, was the man who defeated the Spartans at Marathon, only to lose his fleet at Salamis in the great naval battle of 480 B.C. He is called Ahasuerus in the Bible, and he was the king who married the Jewish maiden Esther.

After Xerxes I, the story of India, Pakistan, and Afghanistan was repeated here in invasion after invasion. The Moslems came in the seventh century with the sword of their faith. The influence of Islam was great, and the people of Iran today are mostly Moslems. Isfahan, which was several times the capital of the country, has many lovely mosques.

Kings still rule in Iran, which is the oldest monarchy in the world. The present emperor, Mohammed Reza Shah Pahlavi, called *Shahanshah* (the king of kings), became king in 1941.

THE PEACOCK THRONE

The Shahanshah's throne is called the Peacock Throne. Behind it in the Tehran throne room is another, which people think contains parts of the famous Mogul throne. Originally it was inlaid with thirty million dollars worth of pearls, emeralds, and rubies. Two peacocks spread their tails across the throne, shining with lovely jewels. No one knows what happened to this throne.

ZOROASTRIANISM, SUFISM, AND BAHAISM

We have already heard of Zoroaster, the Persian religious teacher of the seventh and sixth centuries B.C. He believed that good and evil were always fighting each other. There were good spirits and bad spirits in his religion. He taught the immortality of the soul, and the worth of the individual. He thought we could become like God. A fire always burns on the altars of the temples he established, but Zoroastrians do not worship fire.

Among the Moslems a mystic order arose in the tenth century called *Sufism*. It was a literary movement, which attracted some of the greatest of the Persian poets, men like Omar Khayyam, Hafiz, and Saadi. But it was also a philosophical movement which found God in nature, in flowers, and stars, in the beauty of a face, and the expressions of love.

In the nineteenth century *Bahaism* appeared in Persia. This was another Mohammedan sect, which at first was called *Babism*. The founder was Mirza Ali Mohammed, who claimed to be the successor of the older prophets, Moses, Christ, and Mohammed. He called himself the Bab ed-Din (the Gate of Faith). He aroused a great deal of hostility and was finally executed. His teaching, however, was continued by Baha Ullah, who said he was the messenger of God whom the Bab had announced. He spent most of his life in prison. He was followed by his son Abdul Baha. The Bahaists, who live a very simple life, believe that all religions are one. They work for world peace and for the equality of men and women.

THE TRIBES

There are four chief tribes in Iran: the *Kurds*, the *Lurs*, the *Baktiaris*, and the *Ghashghais*. They live in the Zagros Mountains. The ruler of each of these tribes is a king. The ruler of the whole country is the king of kings, the Shahanshah.

The Kurds are found in Persia, Turkey, Iraq, Syria, and Soviet Armenia, as well as in Iran. They are a proud, fearless, independent people. Many of them would like to unite the tribesmen in these different countries and form a single new nation.

The Lurs have two branches, the Lesser Lurs and the Greater Lurs. The Greater Lurs are usually called the *Bactrians*. There are about eight hundred thousand Lurs in the country, and they are very poor. The saying, "I am a Lur," usually means, "I am very poor." They get some of their customs from Zoroaster. When a lamp is lighted and brought into a room, all who are there rise out of respect.

There are about six hundred thousand Baktiaris. About half of them have two homes, one in the hot region below thirty-five hundred feet, the other higher up, above six thousand feet.

There are about five hundred thousand Ghashghais, who are really Turks. They live in the southern province.

These are the most important groups in Iran today.

OIL AND CAVIAR

Iran is the sixth largest oil-producing country in the world. It may be said to float on oil. But the only area yet developed is in the southwest.

Up in the north on the Caspian Sea, fishing is very important. From the sturgeon caught there comes the best caviar in the world.

The moisture that comes from the Caspian Sea makes the whole coastal plain north of the Elburz Mountains green and fertile. Rice, citrus fruits, and tea are grown there. The west and northwest are the great wheat regions. They are called the breadbasket of Iran. Opium is a government monopoly. Iran is one of the world's largest producers. Tobacco is another government monopoly.

There are mineral resources also: iron, copper, lead, zinc, coal, silver, borax, and emeralds.

Iran is famous for its hand-made rugs and carpets.

A REVOLUTION FROM THE THRONE

Ten years ago the Shah of Iran owned 519 villages. Then he decided to start an evolution from the top to prevent a revolution from below. He began to distribute his lands. The last of the royal property has recently been given away to the people. Some forty-two thousand families now till the lands the Shahanshah once owned. In addition to this the throne has purchased lands from the big land-owners and distributed them among the people.

The big land-owners opposed these reforms. So the Shah held a referendum, on which occasion 95 per cent of the people voted for the new plan. This has been described as a "Revolution from the Throne."

THE PERSIAN LANGUAGE

Many of our English words come from the Persian. Divan, taffeta, turquoise, awning, hazard, sash, and khaki are among them. The language is often very picturesque. They have a striking way of expressing their hospitality. They may say, "My hut is poor and dirty, but you may sit in the light of my eyes."

Mortaza Sadeghi is a wide-awake Iranian boy, who likes camping and traveling and mountain climbing. He has been to the top of Mount Demavend in the winter. Zohre Bourbour has lived in Abadan, the great oil center. Her father is with the National Iranian Oil Company. These two young people say to you, "*Ghadam rouyeh tchashm.*" It's a very polite greeting, which means literally, "You may walk on my eyes."

AN IRANIAN BOY

by Mortaza Sadeghi

MY FAMILY

When I was only two years old my father died. He had worked in the British Embassy in Tehran. My parents, my younger sister, and I were living then in a house in the northern part of the city. It was really a suburb of Tehran. I was born there sixteen years ago.

A few years after my father's death my mother married again. I have two half-sisters by this second marriage. My step-father, who was a little older than my mother, is retired now but he gets a pension. I don't live with my mother any longer. Instead I live with my grandparents in a very small house on the grounds of the Community School in Tehran. My grandfather is a gardener there. We have two rooms and a basement. The roof of the house, like many others in the city, is of wood covered with mud.

MY AMERICAN FRIENDS

I used to play with an American friend, whose father was principal of the Community School. The father's name was

John Irvan, and I think his home in America was at Princeton, New Jersey. He was a missionary in the Presbyterian Church, and just now he is home on a furlough. Although I am a Moslem, I used to go to the Presbyterian Church at times with my friend.

PUBLIC SCHOOLS

I was eight when I first went to the Aben Yamin Elementary School, where I studied for six years. Then I changed to the Mehr School, which is a high school. I am now in the ninth class, taking Persian, Arabic, English, history, geography, mathematics, chemistry, physics, biology, algebra, geometry, drawing, and theology. The Arabic I study is the Arabic of the Koran. The school has its own teacher for the Moslem religion.

We have athletic teams at the school, but I'm not on any of them.

Among my studies I like physics best, and I hope very much to become an engineer. If I can pass my examination for an American college, I think Mr. Irvan would help me to go there. Then I'd specialize in physics.

WORK AND STUDY

I get up at six o'clock, and I have breakfast of bread and butter or cheese, and milk. Sometimes I have eggs. Then from six forty-five to seven forty-five I work for the school as a telephone switchboard operator. From eight thirty to twelve we have classes, which are followed by a two-hour lunch period. I bring my lunch to school, but I buy a Coca-Cola. In the afternoon we have more classes from two to four fifteen. Then from five to eight thirty I'm at the switchboard again. We have dinner at eight thirty: soup sometimes, rice, meat, vegetables, salad, and fruit. I drink either tea or water. I do my homework while I'm at the telephone board. Then I often listen to the radio before I go to bed at ten.

MOUNTAIN CLIMBING

On Friday the school is closed and I don't have to work at the telephone. So I usually do some homework, and I often go on picnics with my friends. We have no car, but a friend's father has one, and he often takes several boys off for an outing. The highest mountain in Iran is just on the edge of the city. This is Demavend, 18,550 feet high. With a few of my friends, I have climbed to the top of it. There is a path to the top and many people ascend the mountain. Some go up on animals, but most people go up on foot. There's always snow on the summit.

When we climbed the mountain it was in the winter. It was snowing at the time. On the first day we went up halfway and spent the night in sleeping bags. The next day we went on to the top. Then on the third day we came down all the way. Demavend is a beautiful mountain.

SUNDAYS

Sunday is a holiday, but I never go on picnics then. Sometimes I go to the Presbyterian Church with my friends. I often play basketball too.

TRAVEL AND CAMPING

Five or six of us boys play around together. We have a tent and sleeping bags and we often go camping. We fish too, and the fishing is very good near Tehran. Our long vacation is in the summer, during June and July. During these holidays I've been to a number of places in the north. I went by car to Pahlevi, which is a port on the Caspian Sea. The Caspian Sea is not as salty as the ocean, but the water has a yellowish color and a bitter taste. There are no tides and the sea has no outlet. I've been fishing there, but I didn't catch anything for I forgot my fishing pole. Near the shore of this sea, but a little inland, is another place called Resht, which I have visited since I have friends who live there. I have another friend in the oil city of Abadan and I once spent fifteen days visiting with him there.

OTHER ACTIVITIES

Sometimes I go to the mosque, and my grandfather has prayers at home. I collect stamps and matchbook covers. I know some of the folk dances of my people, but I always wear western clothes. My languages are Persian and English. As I've said, I want very much to go to America later.

AN IRANIAN GIRL
by Zohre Bourbour

MY FATHER IS IN OIL

My father's name is Nostratolah Bourbour. He was born in Hamadan, about two hundred miles west of Tehran. He graduated from the American school in Tehran. At that time there were really two American schools in the city. One was just for American children, the other was for both Iranian and American youngsters. The latter school, which was, of course, the one my father attended, closed about two years ago, but my father was in this school for twelve years, that is, until he graduated. Then he went to work for the National Iranian Oil Company, and he has been with them altogether for twenty-three years. *Baba*, which is our word for father, is in charge of land acquisition. He has to travel all over Iran in connection with the company's property.

Mami was born in Tehran. I was born there, too, fifteen years ago. We are still living in the same place, a single brick house of two stories and six rooms. The roof is covered with mud. I have two younger brothers and one older sister, who is now seventeen and in the middle school, which you call the high school [in America].

WHEN I WAS SMALL

When I was a little girl I played alone most of the time. I played a great deal with dolls and I had a dollhouse. Now I like to play games like tag with other children, both boys and girls. When girls in my country reach the age of seventeen or eighteen, they don't play with boys any more, however.

SCHOOL

I began my schooling at an elementary school near my home when I was six. I was there for three years. Then Baba was transferred from Tehran to Abadan because of the oil wells there. I was nine years old and I stayed in an Abadan school for three years.

Abadan is on Abadan Island in the Shatt al-Arab, which carries the waters of the Euphrates and Tigris Rivers out to the Persian Gulf. You can reach the city by railway, by road, or by air. It's very hot there. Some of the company houses are air-conditioned, but ours was not. One of the girls I played with had an American mother. Her name was Nina Johan Gity Salehi. But I've lost touch with most of the girls I played with there.

When I came back to Tehran I entered the middle school. I had already had six years of elementary school. Now I'm in the second year of middle school.

MY SUBJECTS

I'm taking Arabic, Persian, English, math, chemistry, physics, the history of the world, geography, painting, and drawing. My favorite subjects are math and geometry. At the end of my third year in middle school I can choose the subjects I want to study. Then after the sixth year I want to go to the university. I'd like to be an interior decorator, or a designer of women's clothes; but the University of Tehran doesn't give the courses I want to take. So I'm not sure where I shall go.

FROM THE RISING OF THE SUN

My school day begins at six, but on other days I don't get up until eight. In the summer classes begin at eight, in the winter at eight thirty. I have eggs, bread and butter and cheese, and tea, sometimes meat. I may have some homework to do before school, and it takes me a half hour to walk there. The morning session ends at twelve, and the afternoon session lasts from two thirty to four thirty. I usually take my lunch from home and this may be rice, meat, vegetables, salad, and Pepsi-Cola. We don't have much fish to eat, for Tehran is too far from the sea. If I buy my lunch at the school canteen it's usually sandwiches and a "Pepsi."

At home after school I have tea and bread and cheese. If I'm hungry I may eat something more than that. Then I have an hour or two of homework. Dinner comes any time from seven to nine. We have no television, but some of my friends do, and I often go to their homes to watch it. I don't play any table games at home except ping-pong. Usually I'm in bed by nine, but in the winter I sometimes stay up till twelve. Whenever I have any spare time I study English. Once a week at school we have an hour of sports, baseball, volleyball, and ping-pong. There are school teams, but I'm not on any of them.

HOLIDAYS

Ours is a Moslem country and Friday is a religious holiday, but there is no regular religious instruction in school. On Friday I study my lessons and play with my friends.

Once every week or every two weeks I go to the movies. Most of the films are American and I like good cowboy pictures.

In June and July come our long holidays. Sometimes we rent a house in some other place. Sometimes we go to a hotel for three or four days. I like best to go back to Abadan. It has changed a good deal since I went there, and there are now many amusements for children, and a good cinema.

I've been to the Caspian Sea, to Isfahan, Persepolis, and Shiraz. Isfahan used to be so magnificent that there was a saying, "Isfahan is half the world." It's a big city with about two hundred thousand people living in it. Two of the mosques are wonderful buildings. The Royal Mosque is covered with lovely enameled tiles. There is also the Cathedral Mosque. These two buildings are among the most beautiful in the world, people say. Shiraz is also a very pretty city.

Persepolis is not far away from Shiraz. Now it's just a place of ruins. Sometimes it's called the "Hundred Columns."

12. IRAQ
LAND OF THE TWIN RIVERS

THE GARDEN OF EDEN

In the second chapter of Genesis we read about the Garden of Eden, where the Lord God put Adam and Eve, the man and woman he had created. Among the many trees that were good to look at and good for food were the Tree of Life and the Tree of the Knowledge of Good and Evil. A river flowed out of the garden to divide into four branches.

Where was this Garden of Eden? There are many different theories, some eighty of them. But two of the rivers are clearly identified as the Tigris and Euphrates. All through the Middle East, therefore, people believe that the Garden of Eden was where these two rivers joined to form the Shatt al-Arab, which then went on to empty into the Persian Gulf.

There is a small village there called Qurna, and there on the bank of the Tigris grows a tree which is thought by some to have been the Tree of Life.

THE BEGINNINGS OF WRITTEN HISTORY

There are many reasons to doubt this tale of the Garden of Eden, but there is no question that the land we now call Iraq was the site of a very ancient civilization. The southern part of the great valley was occupied by a non-Semitic people, called the Sumerians. Their own legends say that they had been there from the time of creation. They had important cities. Eridu may date from the eighth millennium B.C. Near by was Ur, which the Bible says was the home of Abraham. This also dates from very ancient times. It was a great and flourishing city by 3500 B.C.

After the fall of Sumeria two other great cultures arose farther north in the valley. One of them was Babylonia, with its great city of Babylon. The terraced gardens of the city, built on an artificial hill and called the Hanging Gardens of Babylon, were one of the Seven Wonders of the World. The Tower of Babel was said to have stood there. One of its most powerful kings was Hammurabi, who ruled about 2100 B.C. His code of laws is one of the greatest of the ancient codes.

Farther north in the valley stood another olden city, Nineveh, the capital of the Assyrian Empire. It was the leader of the ancient world until 612 B.C., when the empire came to an end.

THE TWIN RIVERS

The land between the two rivers used to be called Mesopotamia, which means "between the rivers." Iraq is a very modern name for the country. Both the Tigris and the Euphrates have their sources in the mountains of eastern Turkey. The most easterly river, the Tigris, forms the boundary between Turkey and Syria for a few miles, and then starts on its long southeasterly journey through Iraq. The Euphrates flows out of the mountains of Turkey, cuts across northeast Syria, and runs along, roughly parallel to the Tigris until the two rivers join at Qurna.

Without these twin rivers Iraq would be nothing but a nomad desert. The water of these mighty streams brings the country to life.

THE DESERT AND THE SOWN

A writer describes Iraq as the "desert and the sown." There is either the sandy waste or the cultivated land, nothing else! In the southwest is the Syrian Desert. Almost no rain falls here and the people are nomads. They are constantly on the move, driving their flocks from one waterhole to another.

The rest of the country is the valley of the Twin Rivers. This is one of the richest lands in the whole Middle East. Here it was that wheat, barley, and oats were first acclimated. The land between the rivers was once the granary of the wide-reaching Babylonian Empire. Then invaders came and destroyed the wonderful system of irrigation canals. After that the rains often brought floods and disaster. The greatest problem of the Iraqi government today is to dam up the rivers, control the flooding, and make water available to thirsty crops only when it is needed.

Two other features of the country must be noted. Up in the north are young, jagged mountains. They run from Turkey into Iran. The people of this area have always lived apart from the people to the south of them. At the other end of Iraq, on the long reaches of the two rivers are enormous marshes. Here the swamp Arabs live. Their villages are built on low mounds hidden by tall reeds. The people either wade from one little island to another or travel in shallow-draft boats.

BOUNDARIES

Iraq used to be a part of Turkey. It was taken away from Turkey in World War I, and the League of Nations asked Great Britain to administer it. The country is bounded on the north by Turkey, by Iran on the east, by Saudi Arabia, Kuwait, and the Persian Gulf on the south, and by Saudi Arabia, Jordan, and Syria on the west. It covers an area of about 172,000 square miles, and the United Nations estimated in 1960 that its population was over seven million.

AN ISLAND CULTURE

The marsh Arabs aren't the only people of Iraq who live in little separate communities. All through the land groups of families have built their houses around a spring, or beside a river. Two-thirds of the people live in villages, and there are very few lonely houses. In some ways this may be called an island culture. In the olden days the caravans were like ships that passed from one island to another. Today there are trains and autos and planes that connect these communities, but it's still a kind of island culture.

Most of the houses in the north are made of stone. Elsewhere they are largely made of mud, strengthened with manure and straw. Palm leaves and reeds are used also. Of course, city houses are better built, often of brick or concrete. The roofs of the houses are usually flat and people often sleep there when the weather is hot.

THE CITIES

There are only six cities with a population of over 40,000 each. In the center of the land on the Tigris River is Baghdad, the capital. It has over 550,000 people. This is the romantic city of the *Arabian Nights*. As early as the ninth century it was wealthy and famous. Recently many people have moved from rural districts into the city, which has become extremely crowded. Some years in the season when the Tigris is very dry and low, people build little shacks in the river bed and plant their crops there.

Mosul in the north is the next largest city. It stands on the Tigris just across from the old ruins of Nineveh. This city of about 340,000 was once known for the excellence of its cotton goods. We get our word "muslin" from the name of the city.

Basra in the south has over 200,000 people. A port city on the Shatt al-Arab, it lies about eighty-five miles from the Persian Gulf. This is the center for date-packing. There are over eighteen million date-bearing palms in this part of the country, and dates are a leading export, next to barley and oil. There are oilfields near Basra too.

In the last thirty-five years Kirkuk in the northeast has trebled in size. Here are found Iraq's greatest reserves of oil. In fact, Iraq is located in the largest oil belt in the Middle East. This includes Iraq, Iran, Saudi Arabia, and Kuwait. All these countries may be said to float on an ocean of oil.

THE PEOPLE

The population of Iraq is increasing at a very high rate. The majority of the people are Arabs and Arab-speaking. They are Moslems in religion. The largest minority is the Kurd tribe, which is found mostly in the northern mountains. They raise cattle, sheep, and goats. As we have already pointed out, the Kurds are found in the adjacent countries, and there is a strong feeling of nationalism among them all. They are in a state of constant unrest, and the Iraqi government has tried to suppress this by military action.

Seventy-five per cent of the people are farmers, called *fellahin*. Their life depends on the fertility of the soil. But they are very backward, very primitive. They are afraid of new experiments, for if these experiments fail they know they will starve. "As stubborn as a fellah," is a common saying. Another is, "You can teach a donkey, but not a fellah."

Almost 90 per cent of the farmers are illiterate. Housing is very poor, sanitation almost unknown. There is a vast amount of malaria, hookworm disease, and bilharziasis.

TOWARDS A BETTER DAY

Recently the government in Iraq has been attempting to improve the lot of the people. And since the two rivers are the life of the land, the most important task is to harness these rivers so that there will always be enough water for the people, but never too much in the way of disastrous floods.

The government is fortunate in having a huge income from oil royalties. This money is now being used largely for new and promising programs to help the people. This means new dams and irrigation ditches to bring water to the parched fields when there is too little rain; plans to reclaim land that has become tired through lack of fertilizers, to bring back into cultivation land that has become too salty to use, because it is not properly drained, to make some twenty million idle acres available in addition to the seven million now being tilled. Other programs provide for many new roads, new schools, and new hospitals. The latest five-year plan (1962–1966) calls for the expenditure of 1.58 billion dollars in 248 major projects.

TROUBLED DAYS OF INDEPENDENCE

The British mandate ended in 1932. In that year Iraq became a sovereign state and a member of the League of Nations. The first king was Emir Faisal who died in 1933. His successor, Ghazi Ibn Faisal, was killed in an auto accident in 1939. The next king was Faisal II, who was assassinated by the so-called Free Officers in 1958. The leader in this coup, Brigadier General Abdul Karim Kassim was himself assassinated in February, 1963, and another officer, Colonel Abdel Solam Aref, took his place.

Zaim Mouhan Khairallah is the son of a sheikh, who was the head of a tribe in the southern region descended from Abraham. Khory Sliwa comes from the other end of the country, from the mountains of the north. She was brought up among the Kurds, who are Moslems, but she is a Nestorian Christian.

MY FATHER WAS A SHEIKH

by Zaim Mouhan Khairallah

MY FATHER'S ANCESTORS CAME FROM YEMEN

Yemen is a little land between the desert and the Red Sea in the southwestern corner of the Arabian Peninsula. One of my ancestors traveled with his caravan across the burning sands of Saudi Arabia and settled in the valley of the Tigris and Euphrates near the head of the Persian Gulf, which the Iraqi call the Arab Gulf. My ancestor went there because the two rivers provide plenty of water. There was very little in Yemen.

In the province of Nasiriya, near the tiny town of Rfai, my grandfather, or my great-grandfather, took possession of a large tract of land that no one was using. This became the property of his descendants. My father had a quarter of a million *donums* (a *donum* is about two-thirds of an acre) and employed hundreds of workers to take care of the land and raise crops for him. My father's name was Mohan Khairallah.

The major crop my father grew was rice. When the rice was harvested he used to bring it to Baghdad in trucks to sell in the market. As the sheikh of his tribe, he was an important person. Toward the end of his life he was elected to Parliament and then he moved to Baghdad with his family, though he used to spend much of his time at Rfai.

SHEIKHS AND PEASANTS

Sheikhs are not elected. The title is handed down from father to son. But if the people don't like the ruling sheikh, it's very easy to get rid of him and to put another man in his place. All the sons of the sheikh are sheikhs themselves, and in the old days I would have been a sheikh too, but the title doesn't mean much now.

The peasants who worked for my father built their own mud huts and got a share of the crops they grew. The share depended on several things. If the land was irrigated and the sheikh pumped the water through it, or if the sheikh provided the seed, the peasants received something like one-third of the crop. If, however, the land was watered by the rains the peasants might get as much as 90 per cent of the winter crop, as well as half the summer crop if the landlord had to furnish the water.

The landlords used to do many other things for the peasants. They often lent them money to tide them over a bad season, and they helped them in all kinds of difficulties.

There were no schools on my father's property, but there were very few schools even in Baghdad at that time.

THE REVOLUTION AND THE LAND REFORM

The revolution that overthrew the young king Faisal and the monarchy took place in 1958, but my father did not live to see it. He died in 1956. All the land of the big owners was taken away from them except a thousand donums for each child. The government also agreed to pay something for the land they took and each child will finally get his share of that.

I now receive a little of this money every year. Out of my share the government will also pay for my education and buy a house for me if I need it. The government may turn over my thousand donums in 1964, and then I can probably put a farmer on the land and grow crops for myself. I won't get all my money until 1968.

MY MOTHER CAME FROM PALESTINE

My father had three wives and my mother was the youngest of them. She was born in Palestine, where for a while her father had a newspaper in Jaffa. Afterwards he was a teacher there. He had been born here in Iraq, but he was not an Iraqi. My mother had four sisters and two brothers. Her mother had some land in Palestine, but when the trouble began there, she sold it to a Jew. When actual fighting finally came in 1948, the whole family left Palestine in a truck. They went to Lebanon. Before they left the Jews tried to kill my grandmother's brother, but he got away.

My mother's two brothers stayed on in Lebanon for schooling. The rest of the family went on to Rfai, and here it was that my mother married the sheikh. I have seven brothers and six sisters but not all by my mother. I have a half-brother who is as old as my mother. My youngest brother has a B.A. from Stanford University in California and is now studying at the University of Chile in Santiago. My mother is now the headmistress of a kindergarten in Baghdad.

I WAS BORN IN BAGHDAD

When my father was elected to Parliament, he got a house in Baghdad in the district called Sa'adoon. It was not far from the White House, where the government entertains some of its guests. While they were there I was born in a hospital thirteen years ago. The house was a single house with five or six rooms in it. There was a big garden for flowers and fruit trees and another house for the servants.

SCHOOLS IN EGYPT AND IRAQ

My first school was in Alexandria, Egypt. This was then called Victoria College, named for the Queen of England; but recently the name has been changed to Victory College. I was sent there because this school was considered to be the best school in the Middle East. Another reason was that one of my aunts married an Egyptian who commanded an Egyptian submarine. He's now the naval attaché for Egypt in London.

Even though Victoria College is a Christian school, it has a mosque for Moslem boys like myself; so we could study the Koran there.

I was in school at Victoria for about five years. I came home for a visit in 1958 and then went back again. But when I came home in 1960 the government would not let me return.

So then I entered Mansur Primary School, which is on the west side of the Tigris River, but still within the city of Baghdad. I was there for about two years and then went to Baghdad College, where I am now in the first form.

My studies are Arabic, English, algebra, history, geography geology, and national education (civics). I am very fond of algebra, and later I'd like to be an oil engineer.

During the breaks between classes we have sports, baseball, football, and tennis.

FREE TIME

Our long vacation comes from June 3 to the end of November. Then I sometimes go to Lebanon and sometimes back to Alexandria. I like the latter place very much, because of the many fine beaches there. I've also been across the border into Jordan, to the island of Bahrein, and to Qatar. My uncle has a chicken farm in the latter place.

On Sundays I usually go to the movies. I like any good ones. I used to fence in Egypt, but there is no fencing in Iraq. I like to read very much, especially English comics. At home we often play monopoly.

THE SHEIKH'S COSTUME

I have a costume I would wear as a sheikh but, of course, I don't wear it much now. The costume has a long robe that reaches my ankles, on top of which I wear an ordinary coat. Then on that I wear an *abaya*, which is another long robe open all the way to the ankles in front. Around the neck of this robe and part way down the front on each side is a wide gold fringe. Then on my head I wear a dark-colored scarf in the winter and in the summer a light-colored one. Finally there is the *agal*, a kind of crown that goes twice around the head over the scarf. In the case of a sheikh this is always gold or silver.

MY RELIGION

Though I am a Moslem I seldom go to the mosque. We have prayers at home but not regularly. I study the Arabic of the Koran. I speak Arabic, English, and a little French.

MY FATHER WAS A FARMER
by Khory Sliwa

MY HOME IS IN THE MOUNTAINS

I was born in Daoudiya, a small village in the northeastern part of Iraq. About a hundred people live there and another village is close by. The mountains around us are high and the villages are in the valleys. There's a small bus that comes from Mosul to our village, but people travel a good deal on donkeys.

All the people wear long baggy trousers, even the women. But the women wear long robes over them. A big cloth belt is wound around the waist, and another cloth around the head for a turban. Each woman has a big scarf that falls down in back, comes over the shoulders, and ties in front.

My father was born in a bigger place near Mosul, but my mother was born in Daoudiya. I was born there too. I don't know just when, but it was probably fourteen years ago.

There are seven girls and three boys in the family, and I'm the second oldest girl. My father's brother, who lives with us, has four girls and one boy. Then my grandmother lives with us too. That makes twenty of us.

THE FARM

All twenty of us live together in a single two-room house. It's made of mud except for the roof beams, and they are covered with mud too. We get our water from a spring in the village and we cook our meals over a wood fire outdoors. We have no toilet and we get our light at night from gasoline lamps.

My father's farm is very small, maybe a quarter of an acre in size. The farmers in the valley grow barley, wheat, apples, pomegranates, peaches, melons, and watermelons. They have vegetables like tomatoes, cucumbers, string beans, and squash. There's no irrigation in our part of Iraq. We get snow in the winter and rain in the summer, and usually we have enough water. My father has forty sheep and ten goats.

WE ARE CHRISTIANS

All the people in our village are Christians. We are called Nestorian Christians. The founder of our religion was a saint called Nestorius. A long time ago he was the Patriarch of Constantinople, but then he was driven out of the church. They tell me there are many Nestorians in Turkey, Iran, and in the north of Iraq. The whole region is usually called Kurdistan. But my people are not Kurds. The Kurds are Moslems and speak a different language, called Kurdish. Our language is Sureth.

OUR CHURCH

Until a few months ago we had a little mud church in our village. There were no pictures or images in it, just the Christian cross. Our people honor the Virgin Mary, but they don't believe that she was the mother of God. Our religion came to us from the church in Mosul, but now we have our own bishop. The bishops in our church are never married.

MY LIFE IN DAOUDIYA

I have many things to do: I go to the spring to fetch water; I help my mother with the children and the housework; I help my father take care of the sheep and work the land; and I play catch with the other children.

There's a government school in the village. I went through four grades there. I studied Arabic, arithmetic, history, reading, and writing. The priest comes to the school to give us religious instruction. All the teachers are Christians, and the teaching is in Arabic. Of course, I learned Sureth at home, but I know Kurdish, the Moslem language, also. We all go to church three times on Sunday.

There is a small airport near my village. King Faisal, before he was killed, used to land there and then travel by road to his summer home in the mountains. Many people come to that part of Iraq in the summer because the climate is so pleasant. In the middle of the day it gets very warm, but the mornings and evenings are wonderful.

OUR VILLAGE WAS BOMBED

Last year there was trouble between the government and the people of the north. So the government sent planes to bomb our village. The people fled. Our family walked for three days with the things we could carry. Then an uncle who has a car picked us up and took us to Mosul. From Mosul we traveled to Baghdad in a truck.

IN BAGHDAD

Now we are in Baghdad for a little while. We found a room to live in that opens on a courtyard. Eleven families live around this courtyard, and all twenty of us sleep in that one room. We have a single cupboard and one bed. Most of us sleep on mattresses which we place on the floor and roll up in the daytime. For this one room we pay eight dinars a month (about twenty-two dollars).

My father got a job as a bellboy in a hotel, my mother went to work as a servant, and I got a job in the kitchen of the Presentation Convent, which is run by the Catholic sisters. At first I didn't know how to use a broom, for our floors are of mud and we just sprinkle them with water. But now I have learned how to do many new things. I clean the vegetables, wash the dishes, and help with the cooking. I come at seven in the morning and leave at two in the afternoon. The sisters give me my breakfast and my lunch. They also give me clothes and food to take home to my family besides my pay. So I like it very much and I hope I can stay here. I don't want to go to school any more. I'd like to become a cook and then I could earn more money.

My father didn't like his work at the hotel. Somehow he learned about our village. He was told that the church had been destroyed by the bombing, but that our house was still standing. He was afraid that the Kurds would take our house, so he decided to go back north again. He left a month ago with my older sister, and we haven't heard from them since then. My mother is staying with us for the time being and a younger sister has also found a job in Baghdad. Maybe the whole family will return to Daoudiya; I hope I can stay here, even though it gets very hot in the summer.

13. SYRIA

CROSSROADS OF
THE ANCIENT WORLD

THE OLDEST CITY IN THE WORLD

The Iraqi say that Baghdad is "the oldest continuously inhabited city in the world." Then when you travel from Baghdad to Damascus you find the Syrians calling Damascus "the
oldest continuously inhabited city in the world." But if you
continue to travel westward to Lebanon you will find the
Lebanese calling Jebail, which stands on the ruins of Byblos
near Beirut "the oldest continuously inhabited city in the
world."

In those dim days of a faraway past it is difficult to settle
any question of priority. Not even the archaeologists can possibly be sure. But certainly Damascus, the capital of present-
day Syria, which the Arabs call Dimishq, has a very ancient
history.

ABRAHAM AND PAUL

In the fourteenth chapter of the Book of Genesis we read that Abram, or Abraham, armed his servants and fought a battle near Damascus, where he rescued Lot, his brother's son, from the hands of unfriendly kings who had taken him prisoner. Damascus, therefore, existed before the time of Abraham, the founder of Judaism.

We hear about Damascus in the New Testament also. In the ninth chapter of the Acts of the Apostles we read that a young man named Saul, who had taken part in the stoning of Stephen, set out with letters from the high priest that he might seize the Christians of Damascus and bring them bound to Jerusalem. On the way he was converted. When he reached Damascus he found a lodging in the street called Straight, and began to preach the gospel of Christ, whose followers he had previously persecuted in the synagogues. Then the Jews of the city plotted to kill him as he went out through the gates of the city. The disciples heard of this and let him down over the wall in a basket.

You can still visit the street called Straight in Damascus and see the place where he was let down over the wall. From the time of his visit to Damascus, Saul was known as Paul, the most famous apostle of early Christianity.

THE GLORY THAT WAS DAMASCUS

For many centuries Damascus has been an important and splendid city. It stands on the Barada River and just outside the city on the edge of the desert are lovely orchards of almonds, figs, pomegranates, and apricots.

Inside the city the bazaars have always been famous. They

sold silks, woolens, and furniture inlaid with mother-of-pearl. Damascene swords were noted for their strength and keenness. We are all familiar with damask tablecloths, which get their name from the city.

THE CROSSROADS OF THE ANCIENT WORLD

The old city of Damascus was important for one special reason. It was situated at the crossroads of the ancient world.

It lay in the center of the Fertile Crescent. This was a great arc of rich land that stretched north along the shore of the Eastern Mediterranean through the region now occupied by Israel, Lebanon, and Syria, then eastward to the mountains of southern Turkey, and then southeastward through the basin of the Tigris and Euphrates until it reached the Persian Gulf. The Fertile Crescent was a natural highway from Egypt and Asia Minor to what is now Iraq. It led onward also to Persia, Afghanistan, and India. It was the route that would-be conquerors took, the route of the trading caravans. When you traveled from the Mediterranean eastward in those days you were very apt to pass through Damascus. If you were a trader you were almost certain to pass that way.

Damascus had wealth, too, and this was a temptation to its neighbors. Whenever any neighbor became strong in Asia Minor, Egypt, and Mesopotamia, its envious eyes turned toward the riches of Damascus. When in addition there were strong nations on two sides of Damascus, Syria became a battleground.

A HISTORY OF STRIFE AND CONFUSION

So through its long history Syria was usually held by foreign powers. From the nineteenth to the thirteenth centuries

B.C. the Hittites ruled it most of the time, but the Egyptians were often there also. The first great native culture to be born within the land was the Phoenician, but this was mostly in what we now call Lebanon. The Phoenicians became a great maritime power and flourished after 1250 B.C. They had trading centers along the coast, though there were no good natural harbors there. After the Phoenicians came the Assyrians and the Babylonians; then the Persians, the Greeks, and the Romans. The Arabs arrived with their new gospel in the years between 633 and 636 A.D., and the people of Syria were largely converted to Mohammedanism.

Toward the end of the eleventh century, the Crusaders came, determined to drive the "infidels," as they called the Moslems, out of the holy places. They were defeated by Saladin, the great Moslem warrior who lived for ten years in Damascus.

So it went on, with one invader after another: the Mamelukes, who were the slave sultans of Egypt, the Mongols from China, the Ottoman Empire from Turkey. Napoleon I brought the French into Syria, and after the First World War France received from the League of Nations a mandate to administer the former Turkish *sanjaks*, or districts, of Damascus, Aleppo, and seven others. These sanjaks were divided into two states, Syria and Greater Lebanon.

The mandate lasted from 1920 to 1941. In 1941 both Lebanon and Syria became independent republics.

ANCIENT AND MODERN BOUNDARIES

In olden times Syria included not only the modern states of Syria and Lebanon but also the land occupied by Palestine.

Ancient Syria was therefore the land where Judaism grew to manhood as well as the birthplace of Christianity.

Today Syria is bounded on the north by Turkey, on the east by Iraq, on the south by Jordan and Israel, and on the west by Lebanon and the Mediterranean. It lies between the Mediterranean and the Syrian and Arabian Deserts. It has an area of 72,000 square miles, and a population of over 4.5 million.

The Syrians call their country *Souriya.*

THE NATURE OF THE LAND

The coastline is one of the straightest in the world. There is hardly a harbor worth mentioning. Latakia is the most important coastal community, but most of the exports actually pass through Beyrouth in Lebanon. Separating Israel from Lebanon are the Anti-Lebanese Mountains. The highest point is Mount Hermon, which rises to nine thousand feet. There are other mountains in the northwest and in the south of Syria. In the south there is also a plain that stretches westward to the Sea of Galilee and the Jordan Valley. There are deserts in the center and the southeast.

Two important rivers flow through the land. The Euphrates runs southeast from Turkey on its way to the Persian Gulf. The Orontes runs north to Turkey.

THE PEOPLE

The people are of Arab origin and speak Arabic. About three-fourths of them are Moslems, and the rest are Christians and Jews. In the Syrian Desert several tribes of Bedouins wander about, and in the south there is a separate Moslem sect called the Druses.

Outside of Damascus and the other principal cities the people are mostly pastoral and agricultural. They have many cattle and camels, sheep and goats. The main crops are wheat, maize, millet, barley, vegetables, figs, apricots, and olives. Near Latakia in the northwest a good deal of tobacco is grown.

THE UNITED ARAB REPUBLIC

The Arabs like to think that the Arab fatherland extends from the Atlantic Ocean to the Persian Gulf. With the exception of Israel all of these countries are Moslem and Arab. Most of the people in these dozen or so nations have long dreamed of a great Arab Union. Recently the leader in the movement to realize this dream has been Gamal Abdel Nasser, the President of Egypt. At last on February 1, 1958, Egypt and Syria agreed to form a United Arab Republic. No longer were there to be citizens of Egypt and citizens of Syria. There was to be a single republic, of which Syria became the northern region and Egypt the southern region. Nasser was chosen President. But many people in Syria did not like to play second fiddle to Nasser. On September 30, 1961, a military coup took place in Syria, and the country declared its independence again.

Another attempt to unite the two countries was made in 1963, but once more the union quickly fell apart.

Nabil Othman Istaz is the son of a former bank president. He likes to write poetry. Huda Siada's father runs buses across the desert between Damascus and Baghdad. She wants to be a pharmacist.

A SYRIAN BOY

by Nabil Othman Istaz

MY FATHER AND MOTHER

My father died in 1961 at the age of sixty-five. He was a banker. At first he was stationed at a government bank in Damascus, but then he was transferred to one of the government's rural banks in Aleppo, where he was the president. After that he was brought back to Damascus, but finally he got sick and had to retire. The bank paid him a pension as long as he lived, and still pays something to the family.

Both my parents were born in Damascus, but there were no children until after my father came back from Aleppo. There are seven children now. I have one older brother and five younger sisters. My brother is twenty-two and works at the Damascus airport, where he is in communications. My two youngest sisters are twins, but not identical.

MY CHILDHOOD

I was born in Damascus fifteen years ago, but in another house not far away from our present home. We now live in the basement of an apartment house with three families living above us. We have three rooms and a large hall that we use as a living room. We own another house from which we get some rent.

When I was younger, I used to have a lot of fun playing in a sandbox, making little houses, and mountains, and rivers, and roads. I played catch and ping-pong, too. My sisters played with dolls. I used to run errands for my mother.

PRIMARY AND SECONDARY SCHOOLS

I started in school at seven. This was a public primary school and I was there for six years. Now I'm in the second year of secondary school. I study Arabic, English, history, geography, national education (civics), painting, music, and religion. I am a Moslem. The subjects I like best are science and English. When I finish school I'd like to work at the airport, but I don't want to be a pilot. I'd like to work on the ground.

MY SCHOOL DAY

My school day begins at six and after I've cleaned up and dressed, I do some homework. I don't eat any breakfast. I'm in school at eight; during the summer, school continues until one and we have no afternoon session. In the winter we go from eight to twelve in the morning and from two to four in the afternoon. At school I may have a sandwich, or a piece of cake, or some candy, and tea to drink. But during the summer I have my lunch at home. I have meat, rice, vegetables, salad, fruit, and tea. After that I usually take a nap until five in the evening. Then I may go out to play or I may do some homework. Dinner comes at eight and it's like my lunch but a little lighter. I listen to the radio and I'm in bed about ten or eleven.

We have sports at school. All of us have physical exercises and then each of us chooses some special sport which he likes. I chose basketball, but other boys play volleyball and soccer. We have school teams, but I'm still too young to play on them.

HOLIDAYS

There's no school on Friday. When I'm preparing for my examinations I study them, but the rest of the year I just have a good time. I may visit my friends and relations, or go on picnics either in a bus or in a friend's car. I go to the movies about three times a week, and I like the exciting films, cowboy movies and adventure stories.

We have a three-month vacation that begins on June 15. But I always get a job then. I've been working in a store that sells and repairs electrical equipment. But I just sell.

MY TRAVELS

When my father was alive the whole family drove over the mountains to Beirut in a car and stayed there for a month. Many people all over the Near East go to Beirut for vacations when they can.

We went to Aleppo also and to some other towns in Syria.

POETRY IS MY HOBBY

Whenever I have any spare time I write poetry. I like to write descriptions of scenery and narrative poems. I took some of my poetry to my schoolteacher once, but she didn't encourage me so I didn't take any more. Now when I like something I've written I give it as a present to a friend. I don't keep any copy for myself.

A SYRIAN GIRL
by Huda Siada

MY FATHER RUNS A BUS COMPANY

My father's name is Bashier Siada. He takes passengers in his buses from Damascus to Baghdad. He has about six buses and some of them are huge trailer buses. There's a paved asphalt road all the way across the desert from Syria to Iraq. My father has been in this business for twenty to thirty years. He has a great handicap, however. He is deaf in both ears. Still he has no difficulty in the family and seems to be able to manage his business successfully. He is very good in arithmetic, and he is really a very remarkable man. He amuses himself by reading a great deal.

THE FAMILY

My parents were both born in Damascus, and I was born here too, in a house not far from the center of the city. We are living in another house now nearer Mount Kassioun. This mountain rises at the edge of the city and has a television station on the top of it. We have an apartment of about six rooms on the third floor.

My oldest brother is twenty. He is in the last year of a private secondary school. For six years he went to an American school in the city, but this was given up. Another brother is nineteen; he and I both go to the public schools.

NURSERY, ELEMENTARY, AND HIGH

From the time I was three until I was old enough to go to a public school at seven I went to a private nursery school. Then I entered the elementary school. At present I'm in the second grade of the high school. My subjects are Arabic, English, history, geography, geology, science, math, art (needlework), public education (civics), domestic science, and religion. I speak Arabic and some English. Most of my teachers are women, but we have a male teacher for religion.

I like mathematics best, and I'd like to become a pharmacist. I could prepare for this at the University of Damascus.

WHEN I WAS SMALL

As a little girl I loved to play with dolls, and I used to make dresses for them. I had a dollhouse too. At nursery school I stayed until three in the afternoon, and I had my lunch there. There was a school bus that carried the children between the school and their homes.

SECONDARY SCHOOL NUMBER TEN

This is also called the high school. In the summer classes are from seven in the morning to two in the afternoon. In the winter they are from eight to twelve on Sunday, Tuesday, and Thursday, with an afternoon session from two to four on Saturday, Monday, and Wednesday. Friday is a holiday.

I get up at six thirty and have bread, cheese, butter, jam,

and sometimes eggs for breakfast. I drink either milk or tea. Then I walk to school. My lunch at home consists of soup, meat, rice, vegetables, salad, and fruit, with water to drink. My favorite foods are fruit and fried meat. When I have my lunch at school, it is usually a sandwich I buy there.

After school I take a nap, help my mother, study for about two hours, watch television for an hour, and read a bit. We have dinner about eight and I go to bed about nine.

On Fridays I help my mother with the housework and do needlework. In the afternoon I may go out with my parents, my brothers, and friends. We may go to the cinema or drive to some favorite place and eat out.

We have a school uniform. It's a dark blue skirt with a light blue blouse, over which we wear a dark blue sweater. We are not allowed to do up our hair in any fancy way.

VACATIONS

We have a winter vacation from the first to the fifteenth of February, and a long three-month vacation in the summer. We have a house in the Anti-Lebanon Mountains. In the summer we spend about a month and a half there. The famous cedars of Lebanon grow on these mountains and many little villages lie on the slopes. My father comes as often as he can, but when he leaves Damascus my older brother goes back to take his place. The rest of the family stays there all the time.

Even in the winter when there's snow on the mountains we may go up for a day or two at a time. We get a very lovely view from our house.

OUR RELIGION

We are Moslems but we don't have regular prayers at home and I don't go to the mosque. We do observe all the festivals.

We fast during *Ramadan* and we feast on the two happy festivals that follow. *Al-Fitr* comes immediately after Ramadan, and *Al-Adha* comes a few weeks later.

MY HOBBIES

I like to cook and I like my needlework. The whole family plays cards together at home. I read a good deal too, particularly the lives of great men, and I like to see detective films.

TRAVELS

I have taken two long trips with my family. One was to Aleppo in northern Syria. This city is in the basin between the Orontes and the Euphrates rivers, and it gets water from the Euphrates. There are many curious bazaars there and a mosque where Zacharias, the father of John the Baptist, is supposed to be buried. There are a good many Jews and Christians in the city as well as Moslems. Aleppo used to be a very important trading center. That was before ships began to sail around the Cape of Good Hope, and before the Suez Canal was built.

Another time I went over the mountains to Beirut, the capital of Lebanon. There are more Christians than there are Moslems in Beirut. It's a beautiful ride over the mountains, and if you want, you can visit Baalbek on the way. There are very famous ruins at Baalbek, including those of a great temple that was destroyed by earthquakes. There's a big stone there, built into a wall twenty feet above the ground. It's more than sixty feet long, fourteen feet wide, and eleven feet thick. I wonder how they ever moved it to its present position. The Greeks and the Romans used to hold this place.

There's another long journey I'd love to make, and that's to America.

SYRIA

Nabil Othman Istaz

Huda Siada

AFGHANISTAN

K

Rohafza and Rohliga Feroz

Zia Ullah Shirzada

Azra Sh

IRAQ

Zaim Mouhan Khairallah

IRAN

Mortaza Sadeghi

Khory Sliwa

PAKISTAN

Zohre Bourbour

Taugeer Ahmad Quraishi

INDIA

INDIA

Rajendra Prasad Misra

Roshmi Roy

Narayana Murthy

Tina Vakil